AF335708

Śikṣāṣṭakam

Swāmī B. V. Tripurāri

Śikṣāṣṭakam
of Śrī Caitanya

Mandala Publishing

For philosophical inquiries contact:

Audarya
22001 Panorama Way
Philo, CA 95466
audarya@swami.org
www.swami.org

To order this and other Mandala Publishing books contact:

Mandala Publishing
17 Paul Drive
San Rafael, CA 94903
1.800.688.2218
www.mandala.org

Cover artwork by Dhīra-lalita dāsī.

The initial inspiration to write a commentary on *Śikṣāṣṭa-kam* came to me as I completed a series of talks on Śrī Kṛṣṇa Caitanya's eightfold teaching in the summer of 2004. The talks took place in the Finnish archipelago, where the days are so long during the summer months that night never fully eclipses the sun. Amid abundant light, darkness cannot enter. As we basked in the light of both the sun and *Śrī Śikṣāṣṭakam*, it was as if neither darkness nor ignorance had any influence.

On returning to California, those who attended the *Śikṣāṣṭa-kam* discourse encouraged me to write a commentary on Gaura's eight verses. Initially I hesitated, but then I discovered that in the over five hundred years since the verses of *Śikṣāṣṭakam* were spoken, very little had been written on them. Although Śrī Rūpa's *Padyāvalī* includes Mahāprabhu's verses along with others under general headings, he doesn't comment on them or even arrange them in any particular order. Śrī Kṛṣṇadāsa Kavirāja's *Śrī Caitanya-caritāmṛta* is the first to give the verses of *Śikṣāṣṭakam* an order and a historical setting: in the Kavirāja's narrative Mahāprabhu speaks them to Rāya Rāmānanda and Svarūpa Dāmodara at the very end of his manifest *līlā*. Kṛṣṇadāsa Kavirāja also explains the verses ever so briefly. I was surprised to find that since the time of Śrī Rūpa and Kṛṣṇadāsa Kavirāja, it was not until the appearance of Ṭhākura Bhakti-vinoda's *Śrī Sanmodana-bhāṣyam* at the end of the nineteenth century that there was any further explanation of *Śikṣāṣṭakam*'s significance.

After considering how little had been written on *Śikṣāṣṭakam* since the time of Mahāprabhu and the fact that it was in our lineage that the most significant commentary had appeared, I put my initial hesitation aside. Studying Bhaktivinoda Ṭhākura's commentary, I felt that out of his mercy he had left some service for his followers to take up in the form of elaborating on his illustrious *Śrī Sanmodana-bhāṣyam*. As those familiar with the writing of Ṭhākura Bhaktivinoda would expect, his work is very original. Perhaps the most significant aspect of Ṭhākura Bhaktivinoda's commentary is the parallel he has drawn between each of Gaura's verses and Śrī Rūpa's stages of *bhakti* that begin with initial faith (*śraddhā*) and end with *prema*. He also ties the seven glories of Śrī Kṛṣṇa *saṅkīrtana*, which are stated in the first verse of *Śikṣāṣṭakam*, to the seven subsequent verses, envisioning the subsequent verses as elaborations on those glories. These are remarkable insights.

After writing *Śrī Sanmodana-bhāṣyam*, Ṭhākura Bhaktivinoda also stressed the relationship between *Śikṣāṣṭakam*'s eight verses and the stages of *bhakti* in his *Bhajana-rahasya*, a text that teaches one how to meditate on *Śikṣāṣṭakam* as one progresses spiritually. By pointing out this relationship in both *Śrī Sanmodana-bhāṣyam* and *Bhajana-rahasya*, Ṭhākura Bhaktivinoda emphasizes the importance of knowing one's level of eligibility, something he equates with true beauty inasmuch as it is unbecoming to think oneself more qualified than one is. Because of this emphasis, Ṭhākura Bhaktivinoda's elucidation on *Śikṣāṣṭakam* serves as a road map to the interior landscape, helping us to determine our goal (*prema*) and then chart our course with spiritual integrity.

The Ṭhākura's commentary was followed by another commentary, *Vivṛtti*, written by the heir to his spiritual legacy, Śrī

Bhaktisiddhānta Sarasvatī Ṭhākura. Sarasvatī Ṭhākura's *Vivṛtti* closely follows the lead of Ṭhākura Bhaktivinoda. The present commentary draws inspiration from Sarasvatī Ṭhākura's *Vivṛtti* in excavating the mine of Ṭhākura Bhaktivinoda's insight. It also guides the reader through Śrī Kṛṣṇadāsa Kavirāja Gosvāmī's brief explanation of *Śikṣāṣṭakam*.

This commentary has been written primarily for those familiar with Gauḍīya Vaiṣṇavism, while also seeking to inform all spiritually inclined persons of the fathomless depth of Śrī Kṛṣṇa Caitanya's contribution. No work is perfect, especially works that deal with spiritual perfection. May the learned devotees point out any faults for my benefit, and may they write more on *Śikṣāṣṭakam* themselves. I pray that all those who helped to bring this commentary to print may be blessed, and that it inspires its readers to tread the path to *prema*.

Swāmī B. V. Tripurāri

The greatest visionary of the Gauḍīya *sampradāya* in recent history, Śrī Kedarnātha Ṭhākura Bhaktivinoda, mercifully revealed the significance of Gaura Kṛṣṇa's *Śikṣāṣṭakam* in his commentary *Śrī Sanmodana-bhāṣyam*. His dearmost follower, Śrīla Bhaktisiddhānta Sarasvatī Ṭhākura, also commented on these eight stanzas. Herein the most insignificant follower of their followers attempts to explore the depths of the ocean of Gaura Kṛṣṇa's poetry, following their inspiration. Should he drown in the process, what will be the loss?

চেতোদর্পণমার্জনং ভবমহাদাবাগ্নিনির্বাপণং
শ্রেয়ঃকৈরবচন্দ্রিকাবিতরণং বিদ্যাবধূজীবনম্ ।
আনন্দাম্বুধিবর্ধনং প্রতিপদং পূর্ণামৃতাস্বাদনং
সর্বাত্মস্নপনং পরং বিজয়তে শ্রীকৃষ্ণসংকীর্তনম্ ॥১॥

ceto-darpaṇa-mārjanaṁ bhava-mahā-dāvāgni-nirvāpaṇaṁ
śreyaḥ-kairava-candrikā-vitaraṇaṁ vidyā-vadhū-jīvanam
ānandāmbudhi-vardhanaṁ prati-padaṁ pūrṇāmṛtāsvādanaṁ
sarvātma-snapanaṁ paraṁ vijayate śrī-kṛṣṇa-saṅkīrtanam

cetaḥ—of the mind; *darpaṇa*—the mirror; *mārjanam*—
cleansing; *bhava*—of worldly life; *mahā-dāva-agni*—
great forest fire; *nirvāpaṇam*—extinguishing; *śreyaḥ*—
of good fortune; *kairava*—the white lotus; *candrikā*—
by the moonbeams; *vitaraṇam*—spreading; *vidyā*—of the
knowledge; *vadhū*—wife; *jīvanam*—the life; *ānanda*—of
blessedness; *ambudhi*—the sea; *vardhanam*—swelling;
prati-padam—at every step; *pūrṇa-amṛta*—of the full nectar;
āsvādanam—giving a taste; *sarva*—completely; *ātma-*
snapanam—bathing of the self; *param*—exclusive; *vijayate*—
triumphs over all; *śrī-kṛṣṇa-saṅkīrtanam*—the congregational
chanting of the holy name of Śrī Kṛṣṇa.

Exclusive Śrī Kṛṣṇa *saṅkīrtana* triumphs over all!
It cleanses the mirror of the mind,
extinguishes the great forest fire of worldly life,
and spreads the white lotus of good fortune
by its moonbeams.
It is the life of the bride named knowledge.
It swells the sea of blessedness,
gives the full taste of deathless nectar at every step,
and bathes the self in all respects.

While pursuing the highest love during his earthly *līlā*, rasarāja Kṛṣṇa was dumbfounded to experience the measure of Rādhā's love, for it exceeded anything that he had ever experienced. Because he always considered himself the king of love, this experience threw Kṛṣṇa into an existential crisis, forcing him to ask the difficult question, "Am I really the king of love, when it is apparent that Rādhā's love exceeds anything that I have experienced?" When the primary reason for his descent—to taste the highest love—was thus frustrated, this in turn affected his ability to accomplish his secondary purpose—to teach the world about love.

To resolve this twofold crisis, Kṛṣṇa, keeping with his nature, attempted to steal the emotions of Rādhā. A clever thief knows where to hide. Where did Śyāma go? That beautiful, dark-complected thief hid himself in the age of darkness, Kali-yuga, disguising himself as a *sādhu*. However, that which he stole was more brilliant than millions of suns. Thus when his devotees—the dearest of Rādhā—looked for him, he was not hard to find.

Realizing the likelihood of his capture at the hands of his devotees, Kṛṣṇa gave away the stolen goods in an effort to deflect attention, advising each person who received the goods to pass them on to another. This, however, only made matters worse, for seeing the distribution of *prema*, his devotees became suspicious. They knew that a love as brilliant as Rādhā's could only be experienced in relation to Kṛṣṇa himself and that he must therefore be in their midst. Furthermore, although Kṛṣṇa had tried to distribute the goods, because of the nature of *prema* it only swelled within him that much more, turning his complexion golden. Attracted by his golden hue and seeing the measure of his *prema*, they dubbed him Gaura Kṛṣṇa and *proceeded to broadcast the truth to the whole world. In the end, this golden Kṛṣṇa, in the captivity of Rādhā's two best friends, wrote his confession in eight stanzas, begging for mercy. Only after receiving that mercy was he able to realize the consequences of what he had done and fully taste Rādhā's love.*

*

Gaura Kṛṣṇa, otherwise known as Śrī Kṛṣṇa Caitanya, is the answer to the existential crisis of *rasarāja* Kṛṣṇa. To maintain his sense of self as the king of love, Kṛṣṇa had to taste Rādhā's love. Therefore he disguised himself as a devotee and pursued the experience of her love. As Gaura, Kṛṣṇa was able to taste the limits of this love. Having fulfilled his primary purpose, he was able to give proper attention to his secondary purpose. Having tasted, he taught and taught well. The essence of his tasting and his teaching is found in his eight stanzas known as *Śikṣāṣṭakam*.

The verses of *Śikṣāṣṭakam* are found in Śrī Rūpa Gosvāmī's collection of verses known as *Padyāvalī*. However, they do not appear there in sequence but are scattered throughout the book. It was Rūpa Gosvāmī's follower, Kṛṣṇadāsa Kavirāja Gosvāmī, who first arranged Mahāprabhu's verses into one piece, as an eight-verse poem in which each sequential stanza represents a progression of spiritual insight.

In *Caitanya-caritāmṛta*, Kṛṣṇadāsa Kavirāja envisions Śrī Kṛṣṇa Caitanya to be in the midst of Rāma Rāya and Dāmodara Svarūpa as he swoons forth his *Śikṣāṣṭakam*. *Śikṣāṣṭakam* is spoken after Kavirāja Kṛṣṇadāsa has completed the entire narration of Gaura Kṛṣṇa's *ācārya-līlā*. Every nuance of Gaura Kṛṣṇa's *līlā* serves as a lesson on love, and just as the curtain is about to close on this drama of divine dispensation, Śrī Kṛṣṇa Caitanya reflects back on its significance in the poetry of *Śikṣāṣṭakam*.

The venerable Kṛṣṇadāsa Kavirāja writes that once Gaura Rāya remained awake the entire night absorbed in a particular *bhāva*, reciting various verses and relishing their significance. Prabhu Gaura joyfully said, "Listen Svarūpa, Rāma Rāya, the sacrifice of *saṅkīrtana* is the means to worship Kṛṣṇa in the age of Kali. Only by this practice do those who are very intelligent attain the lotus feet of Kṛṣṇa."[1] Gaura Rāya then cited what is arguably the most important *abhidheya-tattva śloka* of *Śrīmad-Bhāgavatam* as supportive evidence for his ecstatic insight:

> [In Kali-yuga] those of fine theistic intelligence
> worship him with conviction along with his associates
> through the sacrifice of *saṅkīrtana*.
> With his upraised and ornamented arms as his weapons,
> he constantly utters the syllables *kṛṣ-ṇa*.
> He is Kṛṣṇa (black) yet golden in his glory.[2]

It is in this *Bhāgavata śloka* that Sanātana Gosvāmī found Kṛṣṇa hiding in Kali-yuga, and after citing it, Gaura Kṛṣṇa recited the first verse of his *Śikṣāṣṭakam* in praise of Śrī Kṛṣṇa *saṅkīrtana*.[3]

Paraṁ vijayate śrī-kṛṣṇa-saṅkīrtanam!

In the beginning of his eightfold teaching, Gaura Kṛṣṇa trumpets the virtues of Śrī Kṛṣṇa *saṅkīrtana* in an effort to awaken *śraddhā* (faith) in its efficacy and thus give rise to *śraddhā*'s outward expression of *śaraṇāgati* (surrender). Such faith creates eligibility for treading the *bhakti-mārga*. Divine faith is the beginning of Kṛṣṇa *bhakti*. Filled with such faith, Gaura Kṛṣṇa cries out, "*paraṁ vijayate śrī-kṛṣṇa-saṅkīrtanam*."

The words *paraṁ vijayate* call for exclusive adherence to Śrī Kṛṣṇa *saṅkīrtana*, forgoing any other path. With a similar emphasis on *śraddhā* and *śaraṇāgati*, *Bhagavad-gītā*, Śrī Kṛṣṇa's song to Arjuna, reaches its conclusion. The famous words *sarva-dharmān parityajya mām ekaṁ śaraṇaṁ vraja* bring Śrī Kṛṣṇa's song to a close.[4] Following this conclusion, Kṛṣṇa's life story, *Śrīmad-Bhāgavatam*, begins with the same emphasis. The words *dharmaḥ projjhita-kaitavo 'tra* open the book about his life.[5] Both the closing statement of *Bhagavad-gītā* and the opening statement of *Śrīmad-Bhāgavatam* advocate faith in exclusive devotion to Śrī Kṛṣṇa and the surrender that corresponds with it.

As Kṛṣṇa's concluding words of the *Bhagavad-gītā* are strong yet prefaced by more than six hundred verses justifying them, so too are the opening lines of *Śrīmad-Bhāgavatam* strong yet well supported when they dismiss all other expressions of *dharma* and even the ideal of salvation. The insistence on exclusive devotion in the *Bhāgavata*'s introduction is followed by almost eighteen thousand verses in support of its premise. Similarly, *Śikṣāṣṭakam*'s initial emphasis on *śraddhā* and *śaraṇāgati* has been prefaced by Gaura Kṛṣṇa's entire life of divine love, which speaks louder than precept. Gaura's position is also well supported by the virtues of *nāma-saṅkīrtana* that he lists in the balance of this initial *Śikṣāṣṭakam śloka*, the seven successive verses of *Śikṣāṣṭakam*, and the ocean of scripturally based literary support that the Vṛndāvana Gosvāmīs and their successors churned from Gaura Kṛṣṇa's *Śikṣāṣṭakam*.

Thus from the outset *Śikṣāṣṭakam* promotes faith in the efficacy of exclusive Śrī Kṛṣṇa *saṅkīrtana*. This faith is not blind, dogmatic belief, but rather enlightened faith drawn from revelation. Such faith mandates change in our lives, a change of heart that involves *śaraṇāgati*, the stage on which the drama of *kṛṣṇa-bhakti* is performed. The first six steps on the ladder to *vraja-bhakti*—from initial *śraddhā* to *ruci* (taste)—constitute the process of fully erecting the stage of *śaraṇāgati* within one's heart, thus connecting the ray of faith that first dawns in one's heart with the sun of faith that never sets in the land beyond doubt and misconception. It is faith in the efficacy of Śrī Kṛṣṇa *saṅkīrtana* that situates one on the path, and faith-filled *saṅkīrtana* itself that moves one along.

While Śrī Caitanya glorifies *saṅkīrtana* in an effort to elicit faith in its efficacy, he does not explain the significance of the term *saṅkīrtana*, which, aside from its ordinary meaning, has a special significance for Śrī Caitanya and his followers. Here in *Śikṣāṣṭakam* Mahāprabhu qualifies his *saṅkīrtana*, referring to it as "Śrī Kṛṣṇa *saṅkīrtana*." It is necessary to mine the significance of all four of these words—Śrī, Kṛṣṇa, *sam*, and *kīrtana*—to realize the wealth of Śrī Caitanya's intentions.

Kīrtana means glorification of another. It derives from the verbal root *kīrti*, which means fame. It is that by which one makes the virtues of others well known, and that by which one becomes virtuous oneself. In general, one becomes glorious by praising others, as opposed to glorifying oneself. One can praise another's name, qualities, form, or activities, making for different kinds of *kīrtana*.

Here in *Śikṣāṣṭakam*, Śrī Caitanya emphasizes *nāma-kīrtana*, but not *kīrtana* of just any name. He calls for exclusive *kīrtana* of the name of God, which is considered to be nondifferent from God himself. If there is any difference between Kṛṣṇa and his name, it is that in the form of his name he is more approachable. Śrī Rūpa Gosvāmīpāda has explained this in his *Śrī-kṛṣṇa-nāmāṣṭakam*:

> O Harināma!
> You manifest in two *svarūpas*
> as "named" and "name."
> The name's fame exceeds that of the named.
> What proof is there of this?
> The name's serious offender
> upon becoming a repenter
> through words and worship of this name
> will always bathe in a sea of ecstasy.[6]

Thus in the form of Kṛṣṇa *kīrtana*, Kṛṣṇa *nāma* is both high, being one with God, and highly accessible at the same time.

Mahāprabhu has further qualified his method of *kīrtana*, advocating not only *kīrtana* of the name of Kṛṣṇa but *saṅkīrtana* of Kṛṣṇa *nāma*. *Sam* means full, complete, and comprehensive. The word *saṅkīrtana* implies comprehensive glorification that is both quantitatively and qualitatively so. Glorification is quantitatively complete if it is unanimous—if everyone present participates. Thus *saṅkīrtana* suggests glorification in unison with other like-minded persons, and thereby the association of saintly persons—*sādhu-saṅga*.

The quality of Gaura Kṛṣṇa's *saṅkīrtana* cannot be understood without mentioning Rādhā. The word *śrī* in Gaura's first verse speaks of Kṛṣṇa's divine consort. It is in pursuit of her love that Kṛṣṇa becomes Gaura and sings in *saṅkīrtana*. He sings in her mood, seeing himself through her eyes. No one knows Kṛṣṇa better than Rādhā. Her love is called *samarthā-rati*, competent love. It is capable of completely conquering Kṛṣṇa, and as we shall see from the final *śloka* of *Śikṣāṣṭakam*, it is this kind of love that Śrī Caitanya tastes and distributes in Śrī Kṛṣṇa *saṅkīrtana*: the highest quality of love, Śrī Rādhā's *prema* in *mahābhāva*.

Although *saṅkīrtana* is the *dharma* of Kali-yuga, in the current *yuga* cycle there is a special concession. Not only does Gaura Kṛṣṇa distribute *dharma* in the broadest possible outreach, he distributes the highest quality of *prema*, inviting everyone into the innermost chamber of his own heart. Thus he has woven a wreath out of both *prema* and *saṅkīrtana* and seeks to garland the world with it.[7]

When the *rāja* of Purī first saw the *saṅkīrtana* of Gaura's associates, he was filled with wonder (*camatkāra*). He had never witnessed this kind of *kīrtana*, this kind of dancing, this kind of love.[8] Pratāparudra Mahārāja was no stranger to glorification of Kṛṣṇa. He presided over a city centered on Kṛṣṇa's glorification, a city that was host to millions and millions of pilgrims.

When he asked his brother-in-law what kind of *kīrtana* it was, Gopīnātha replied, *caitanyera sṛṣṭi ei prema-saṅkīrtana*: "This is the creation of Śrī Caitanya. It is called *prema-saṅkīrtana*."[9] Not all forms of *saṅkīrtana* offer *prema*, but the *saṅkīrtana* of Gaura Kṛṣṇa is about *prema* alone. Indeed, it frowns on mere deliverance (*mukti*).

The principal *nāma-mantra* invoked by Śrī Caitanya in his *prema-saṅkīrtana* is mentioned in the *śruti*. *Kalisantaraṇa Upaniṣad* calls this *nāma-mantra* of sixteen names *tāraka-brahma nāma*. *Tāraka* means deliverer, and here it implies that chanting this *nāma-mantra* results in deliverance from *saṃsāra*, especially in Kali-yuga. In fact, this is the *nāma-mantra* that the *yugāvatāra* distributes in the dark age of Kali, the Hare Kṛṣṇa *nāma-mantra*. However, neither the *yugāvatāra* for the age of Kali nor the *Upaniṣads* speak of *prema*.

The special concession of *prema-saṅkīrtana* is a result of Śrī Caitanya's being Kṛṣṇa. He is not the usual Kali-yuga *avatāra*, who appears in the world to deliver people from birth and death by advocating the *yuga-dharma*. He is not an *avatāra* of Nārāyaṇa or Kṛṣṇa but rather Kṛṣṇa himself. Although he does teach the *yuga-dharma*, he has another internal agenda of his own. He does not chant merely *tāraka-brahma nāma* but *pāraka-brahma nāma*. *Pāraka* means "competent." Here it implies that the Hare Kṛṣṇa *nāma-mantra* is competent not only to deliver one from *saṃsāra* but furthermore to give the treasure of *prema*.[10] Thus *Śikṣāṣṭakam*'s phrase *paraṁ vijayate śrī-kṛṣṇa-saṅkīrtanam* heralds the glory of that which is the best form of *sādhana/sādhya*, or spiritual practice that naturally leads to the highest form of spiritual perfection in *prema*. What then is the need for any other *sādhana*, and where can one find a higher *sādhya*?

After praising the paramount spiritual practice with the words *paraṁ vijayate śrī-kṛṣṇa-saṅkīrtanam*, Śrī Caitanya delineates seven effects of *nāma-saṅkīrtana*. In the vision of Ṭhākura Bhaktivinoda, these seven effects correspond with the seven sequential steps that follow *śraddhā* and *sādhu-saṅga* and end in *prema*, as delineated by Śrī Rūpa Gosvāmī in his *Bhakti-rasāmṛta-sindhu*. Śrī Rūpa writes:

> First faith, then holy association,
> followed by the acts of *bhajana*,
> resulting in the cessation of obstacles,
> then steadiness, taste, attachment,
> ecstasy, and divine love.
> This is the order of the stages
> through which *prema* arises in *sādhakas*.[11]

The first two of these steps, *śraddhā* and *sādhu-saṅga*, have already been discussed.[12] After arousing faith in the method of his divine madness and implying that it is best pursued in the company of *sādhus*, Śrī Caitanya has chosen to enumerate seven particular glories of *nāma-saṅkīrtana*, which correspond with the seven steps remaining to attain Kṛṣṇa *prema*. Each of these steps is further described in greater detail in the next seven verses of *Śikṣāṣṭakam*.

Ceto-darpaṇa-mārjanam

Cetaḥ is a Sanskrit word that eludes English translation. It is often rendered as heart, mind, or consciousness. It derives from the verbal root *cit*, which means to know or to become aware. Thus it refers to that internal faculty by which one becomes conscious of oneself. Here Gaura Rāya compares this faculty to a mirror, the mirror of awareness. A mirror has no image of its own but reflects whatever image comes before it. If the mirror of our awareness is affected by material desire, it will project a material image or sense of identity. Śrīman Mahāprabhu has compared such desire and the subsequent image it projects to dust covering the mirror of our awareness.

The *jīva* soul exists, it can be aware of its existence, and it exists for a purpose. The purpose of the *jīva* is to serve and thus love. When its existence is identified with matter (*miśra-sattva*), its lack of awareness of its true self gives rise to a material identity (*ahaṅkāra*), and consequently its purpose remains unfulfilled by serving desires born of material identification (*kāma*). This dust of material motivation can be wiped away, leaving the mirror of our awareness clean.

Cleansing the mirror of our consciousness is the goal of *niṣkama-karma-yoga*, the *yoga* of selfless action. By realizing this goal, the *jīva* no longer identifies with matter (*śuddha-sattva*), it attains knowledge of the self as consciousness (*brahma-jñāna*), and it partially fulfills its purpose, although it is suspended in the joy of identifying with Brahman (*brahmānanda*). However, cleansing the heart is only the initial effect of *nāma-saṅkīrtana*, not the end result. Furthermore, *nāma-saṅkīrtana* cleanses the mirror of our awareness in a way that involves using our head (*su-medhasa*) to soften our heart. It does so by placing the mirror of our awareness before Kṛṣṇa *nāma*, the perfect object of love. This results not only in cleansing the dust of material desire and identification from the mirror of our awareness but further in positioning us to experience a pure state of existence (*viśuddha-sattva*), to become aware of our spiritual identity (*samvit*), and to fulfill our purpose in love (*hlādinī*).

As we shall see in the discussion of the second stanza of *Śikṣāṣṭakam*, association with Kṛṣṇa *nāma* entails coming under the influence of Kṛṣṇa's *svarūpa-śakti*, for Kṛṣṇa *nāma* is filled with his *śakti*. It is only in this condition that the *jīva* can realize its full potential. The first step in this direction is *śraddhā*, followed by *sādhu-saṅga*. After taking shelter of one's *guru* in the context of *sādhu-saṅga*, one receives directives from the *guru* (*bhajana-kriyā*) that set this cleansing process (*anartha-nivṛtti*) in motion. The stages of *bhajana-kriyā* and *anartha-nivṛtti* correspond with the initial effect of *nāma-saṅkīrtana* and are discussed further in verse two.

Bhava-mahā-dāvāgni-nirvāpaṇam

The second effect of *nāma-saṅkīrtana* is deliverance from the great fire of material existence, *bhava-mahā-dāvāgni-nirvāpaṇam*. The metaphor of a forest fire is often employed to help us understand the nature of material existence. Just as a forest fire often has no external cause but ignites on its own by the friction of two trees, similarly the responsibility for the conflagration of material existence rests with the desires of its inhabitants. God is not to blame. *Karma* is the stern hand of nature that responds in kind to any and all forms of exploitation. Nature is not to be exploited by the mind's idea of what her purpose is. She belongs to God.

While a forest fire often starts on its own, it does not stop on its own. Moreover, human efforts to extinguish a forest fire often prove futile, leaving firefighters praying for rain. Similarly, although God is not responsible for the suffering of material existence, only he can bring an end to it. Atonement and the culture of self-knowledge are compared to human efforts to extinguish a forest fire. They are insufficient. Atonement fails to extinguish the fire of desire, and the culture of knowledge attempts to extinguish desire in a way that leaves no room for new growth, no possibility of spiritual desire.

Where human effort falls short, only God can make up the difference. *Nāma-saṅkīrtana* descends from God. Narottama dāsa Ṭhākura writes, *golokera prema-dhana, hari-nāma-saṅkīrtana*: "*Harināma-saṅkīrtana* is Goloka's charity of love."[13] In order that the gift of Goloka's love may be embraced, *nāma-saṅkīrtana* first extinguishes the forest fire of material existence. When by the grace of Kṛṣṇa *nāma* the fire of material desire is extinguished, one's *sādhana* becomes *niṣṭhā*, fixed, even as the smoke of such desire lingers. With both feet still in this world, the *sādhaka*'s eyes are fixed on a vision of Goloka. At this stage one's spiritual practice is both outwardly unflinching and illumined within. The spirit of the *sādhaka*'s practice in this stage is discussed in the third stanza of *Śikṣāṣṭakam*.

Śreyaḥ-kairava-candrikā-vitaraṇam

The phrase *śreyaḥ-kairava-candrikā-vitaraṇam* speaks of *ruci-bhakti*. This is the sixth stage mentioned in Rūpa Gosvāmī's verse detailing the *sādhaka's* development from *śraddhā* to *prema*. Śrī Kṛṣṇa Caitanya describes it here as the third effect of *nāma-saṅkīrtana*. This effect—the stage of *ruci*—will be elaborated on in the fourth verse of *Śikṣāṣṭakam*.

The word *śreyaḥ* speaks of something auspicious and beautiful. Kṛṣṇa *nāma* is that which is most auspicious among all that is auspicious, including other names of God. Gaura Kṛṣṇa has given the world *nāma-śreṣṭham*, the most auspicious and splendidly beautiful conception of the holy name. In this connection Ṭhākura Bhaktivinoda cites the well-known stanza of *Skanda Purāṇa* glorifying the holy name of Kṛṣṇa, *madhura-madhuram etan maṅgalaṁ maṅgalānām*: "Sweetest of the sweet, most auspicious among that which is auspicious."

When the burning effect of the fire of material existence is extinguished by *nāma-saṅkīrtana*, Kṛṣṇa *nāma* begins to benedict his disciple with the cooling moonlike rays of his splendor. These splendorous rays are the *svarūpa-śakti* emanating from Kṛṣṇa *nāma*. Here the *sādhaka's* heart is compared to the white night-blooming lotus, *kumuda*. At the stage of *ruci*, the *sādhaka's* heart is pure like a white lotus, uncolored by the passion of the world. For this reason Mahāprabhu has chosen the metaphor of a white *kumuda* rather than a red one. In *ruci-bhakti*, the heart, previously contracted in the shadow created by lust, begins to bloom in love like the white lotus in contact with the rays of the moon.

The moon's light is reflected light, and here it represents a semblance of actual *bhāva*. In *ruci-bhakti* one is still a *sādhaka*, and the ray of the sun of *prema* that is *bhāva* has not yet dawned in the heart; however, one experiences a semblance of *bhāva* and an uninterrupted taste for chanting and other devotional practices. *Ruci-bhaktas* have no material attachment, yet they are attached to the means to attain *prema*. Their *śraddhā/ śaraṇāgati* are mature, and they have thus erected within their hearts the stage on which the drama of Kṛṣṇa *līlā* will soon be performed.

Vidyā-vadhū-jīvanam

When attachment to the means of attaining *prema* matures, it develops into attachment for the object of *prema*, Śrī Kṛṣṇa, who then appears on the stage of the *sādhaka*'s heart. This developmental stage is called *āsakti*, the final stage of *sādhana-bhakti*. Gaura Kṛṣṇa poetically describes this fourth effect of *nāma-saṅkīrtana* as "the life of the bride named knowledge," *vidyā-vadhū-jīvanam*. This effect will be discussed in greater detail in the fifth verse of *Śikṣāṣṭakam*.

Vidyā is often rendered "practical knowledge," differentiating it from abstract theoretical knowledge. Applied knowledge is devotion, and thus it can also be said that in the final analysis the highest knowledge is *bhakti*. This is Śrī Kṛṣṇa's opinion stated in his opening lines of the *Gītā*'s ninth chapter. There Kṛṣṇa says that he will now describe the king of knowledge, *rāja-vidyā*, and careful study of the chapter reveals that this king of knowledge is unalloyed devotion.

The *śruti* concurs. In *Gopāla-tāpanī Upaniṣad* we find, *gopī-jana-vidyā-kalā-prerakaḥ*: "[Kṛṣṇa] is the master (*prerakaḥ*) of the *gopīs*, who are the potencies (*kalā*) of the knowledge (*vidyā*) that is love characterized by compassion."[14] In other words, the unalloyed love that the *gopīs* embody represents knowledge. Śrī Prabodhānanda Sarasvatī adds, "The cowherd maidens are those who are the parts of perfect knowledge—loving devotion in a particular mood." Commenting on the phrase *vidyā-vadhū-jīvanam* in his *Bhajana-rahasya*, Ṭhākura Bhaktivinoda offers further support to the notion that devotion is pure knowledge by citing *Śrīmad-Bhāgavatam*: "True knowledge is that by which one becomes conscious of Kṛṣṇa."[15] He also quotes the following verse from the *Garuḍa Purāṇa*, which is cited in *Hari-bhakti-vilāsa*:

> O king! If you want to gain the greatest *jñāna*,
> or if you want to go beyond this goal,
> then zealously glorify Govinda.[16]

In Sanātana Gosvāmī's commentary on this verse in *Hari-bhakti-vilāsa*, he writes, "The highest knowledge is the glory of devotion to Kṛṣṇa."

This highest knowledge that is mature devotion to Kṛṣṇa is a manifestation of Kṛṣṇa's *svarūpa-śakti*. Being feminine, this *śakti* is appropriately referred to as a bride. This is what Mahā-prabhu has done here in *Śikṣāṣṭakam*. By saying that Kṛṣṇa saṅkīrtana is the life of the bride named knowledge, he is in ef-fect saying that Kṛṣṇa *nāma*, who is nondifferent from Kṛṣṇa, is the husband of *bhakti*. In fact, the literal translation of the phrase *vidyā-vadhū-jīvanam* is "the life (husband) of the wife called knowledge." Thus Kṛṣṇa *nāma* as expressed in *nāma-saṅkīrtana* is the life of the bride named knowledge, and this bride is Kṛṣṇa's *svarūpa-śakti*, the highest manifestation of which is Śrī Rādhā.

Ānandāmbudhi-vardhanam

As knowledge of one's *svarūpa* manifests, one passes from the final stage of *sādhana-bhakti* into *bhāva-bhakti*. The *sādhya* of *sādhana* is *bhāva*. At this stage the *sādhaka* has pulled up the anchor of material life and is now adrift in a sea of ecstasy. Although the *jīva* remains infinitesimal, in *bhāva-bhakti* it nonetheless experiences infinite bliss in a shoreless ocean of spiritual emotions. Śrī Kṛṣṇacandra *saṅkīrtana* causes this ocean of ecstasy to increase without limit, just as the moon causes the ocean's tide to rise. *Bhāva-bhaktas* are not agitated by the demands of the senses. They are sober people. However, the ecstasy of *nāma-saṅkīrtana* sometimes makes them appear agitated and intoxicated.

Bhāva-bhakti is indicated in the phrase *ānandāmbudhi-vardhanam*: "[Śrī Kṛṣṇa *saṅkīrtana*] increases the ocean of ecstasy." This same phrase is used by Śrīnivāsa Ācārya in his *Ṣaḍgosvāmy-aṣṭakam* when he describes how the Six Gosvāmīs were expert in increasing the ocean of ecstasy through their engagement in *nāma-saṅkīrtana, ānandāmbudhi-vardhanaika-nipuṇau.* Śrīnivāsa goes on to say that these Gosvāmīs saved others from the mere drop of ecstasy found in salvation, *kaivalya-nistārakau.* This statement refers to the fact that *bhāva-bhakti* makes little of salvation (*mokṣa-laghutākṛt*), which is like a drop of water in comparison to an ocean. This effect of *saṅkīrtana* is explained in greater detail in the sixth verse of *Śikṣāṣṭakam*.

Prati-padaṁ pūrṇāmṛtāsvādanam

When the ray of *prema* that appears in one's heart as *bhāva* is properly cultivated through *nāma-saṅkīrtana*, it turns into *prema*. Attaining *prema*, one tastes (*āsvādanam*) the totality (*pūrṇam*) of the nectar of immortality (*amṛta*) at every step (*prati-padam*). This *prema* is first experienced through unbearable pangs of separation from Kṛṣṇa followed by the joy of union. However, at every step, either in union or in separation, the *prema-bhakta* tastes the nectar of immortality.

Immortality is compared to deathless nectar, the fountain of youth. Life beyond death, however, is not the full cup of immortality. The totality of the nectar of immortality involves tasting *prema* forever in a realm where talking is singing and walking is dancing in *nāma-saṅkīrtana*. Thus *nāma-saṅkīrtana*, unlike other spiritual practices, is both *sādhana* and *sādhya*.[17] It is the paramount spiritual practice that not only carries one into eternity but continues to manifest in perfection as *prema-saṅkīrtana*. This *sādhya*—*prema*—is the final glory of *nāma-saṅkīrtana*, and it will be discussed further in the seventh and eighth stanzas of *Śikṣāṣṭakam*.

Sarvātma-snapanam

The limitations of worldly love are not found in *prema*. World-ly love does not involve the soul proper, nor are one's material senses and mind ever satisfied by it. In worldly love the senses are not perfect, but *prema* grants one spiritual senses to facilitate one in satisfying the transcendental senses of Kṛṣṇa. Without such spiritual senses it would be impossible for one to fully taste *prema*. When one attains *prema*, one's senses, mind, and soul are fully bathed in a shower of spiritual love, and thus they become fully satisfied.

The word *ātmā* means body, mind, or soul. Thus *sarvātmā-snapanam* indicates that *nāma-saṅkīrtana* purifies not only the soul but one's body and mind as well. The word *ātmā* can also refer to Kṛṣṇa, the soul of all souls, and in *prema*, not only are his devotees showered with his love, but they also shower Kṛṣṇa with their love.

In *prema*, absorption in one's spiritual identity (*svarūpāveśa*) is complete, as one is immersed in an ocean of the nectar of Kṛṣṇa's service. After uttering the first verse of *Śikṣāṣṭakam*, Śrī Gaurasundara explained this himself to Rāma Rāya and Dāmodara Svarūpa, while summarizing the effects of Śrī Kṛṣṇa *saṅkīrtana*:

> *Saṅkīrtana* destroys sin, *saṃsāra*,
> cleansing one's consciousness.
> It gives birth to all of *bhakti-sādhana*—
> birth to the *sādhya* of *kṛṣṇa-prema*.
> It gives the taste of *prema*'s immortal nectar
> and attainment of Kṛṣṇa,
> thus drowning one in a sea
> of sweet service perpetually. [18]

নাম্নামকারি বহুধা নিজসর্ব্বশক্তিস্-
তত্রার্পিতা নিয়মিতঃ স্মরণে ন কালঃ ।
এতাদৃশী তব কৃপা ভগবান্মমাপি
দুর্দৈবমীদৃশমিহাজনি নানুরাগঃ ॥২॥

nāmnām akāri bahudhā nija-sarva-śaktis
tatrārpitā niyamitaḥ smaraṇe na kālaḥ
etādṛśī tava kṛpā bhagavan mamāpi
durdaivam īdṛśam ihājani nānurāgaḥ

nāmnām—holy names; *akāri*—manifested; *bahudhā*—so many; *nija-sarva-śaktiḥ*—all your power; *tatra*—there (in them); *arpitā*—invested; *niyamitaḥ*—no rule; *smaraṇe*—to recall; *na*—not; *kālaḥ*—hour; *etādṛśī*—so great; *tava*—your; *kṛpā*—mercy; *bhagavan*—O Bhagavān; *mama*—my; *api*—but; *durdaivam*—misfortune; *īdṛśam*—such; *iha*—here (for the holy name); *ajani*— born; *na*—not; *anurāgaḥ*—attraction.

So many names you've manifested,
and in them invested all your power.
There is no hour, no rule to recall them.
O Bhagavān, your mercy is so great!
But just see my fate, my misfortune:
for your name, I have no attraction.

Continuing to trumpet the glories of Kṛṣṇa *nāma*, Śrī Kṛṣṇa Caitanya expresses his amazement with the words *etādṛśī tava kṛpā bhagavan*: "O Bhagavān, your mercy is so great." In the opinion of Mahāprabhu, magnanimous dispensation reaches its zenith with the appearance of Kṛṣṇa *nāma*. Kṛṣṇa *nāma* is so high, so great, yet he nonetheless makes himself so readily available. Although nondifferent from Kṛṣṇa himself, Kṛṣṇa *nāma* is more merciful.

After reciting this second verse of his *Śikṣāṣṭakam*, Gaura Kṛṣṇa began to discuss its significance by explaining to Rāma Rāya and Svarūpa Dāmodara that God has many names because people have many desires.[1] By this we learn that there is a relationship between the desires of the *jīvas* and Bhagavān's names, just as there is between the condition of the *jīvas'* hearts and Bhagavān himself. He reciprocates with the *jīvas* in consideration of their desires. In the *Bhagavad-gītā* Śrī Kṛṣṇa tells Arjuna, "As people surrender to me, I reciprocate accordingly. Everyone follows my path in all respects, O Pārtha."[2]

How many names does Bhagavān have? He has as many names as there are desires in the hearts of *jīva* souls! For that matter, *Vedānta-sūtra* informs us that every word indicating an object or power is first and foremost a name for God:

Words primarily denote God
for he resides in all things,
both the mobile and immobile.
But that words refer to God

28

is only known with time
after hearing from scripture.[3]

Mahāprabhu personally realized this *sūtra*'s import that all words are names of God. In his youth he was renowned for his scholarship and had many students. After he received Vaiṣṇava *dīkṣā* from Śrī Īśvara Purīpāda and learned the conclusions of the *bhakti-śāstra* under his guidance, he began to explain all Sanskrit words designating material objects as primarily referring to Kṛṣṇa and only secondarily to the objects themselves. He identified the particular aspect of Kṛṣṇa residing in each material object that caused it to be called by a particular word. He realized that all words denoting power or energy also refer by extension to their underlying energetic source and that what is desirable in any object is so because of God's presence therein. Baladeva Vidyābhūṣaṇa asserts that such realization is the goal of Vedānta—*vāsudevaḥ sarvam iti*. Commenting in his *Govinda-bhāṣya* on the above *sūtra* he writes, "The object of Vedānta is to give rise to the knowledge that every word is really the name of God."[4]

Although all words are names of God, Gaura emphasizes in this stanza of *Śikṣāṣṭakam* names of Kṛṣṇa that directly refer to Śrī Kṛṣṇa's person, form, qualities, and *līlā*. Mahāprabhu says that Bhagavān Śrī Kṛṣṇa has manifested many names in this world (on the tongues of his devotees) and that these names are filled with all of Kṛṣṇa's personal *śakti*. These names are those that identify him in *līlā* with his devotees—his primary names chanted by his unalloyed devotees. They are names that each of his devotees holds most dear to his or her heart because they correspond with a particular sentiment of love for Bhagavān. Names such as Brahman and Paramātmā, on the other hand, are secondary names of God and do not refer to him in divine play energized by his internal *śakti*.

Kṛṣṇa's unalloyed devotees are embodiments of his *svarūpa-śakti*, in reciprocation with which Kṛṣṇa makes his appearance. Their love—Kṛṣṇa's *svarūpa-śakti* invested into their hearts— causes Kṛṣṇa to appear in a form that corresponds with their purified hearts. Where then does Kṛṣṇa reside? He resides in the hearts of his devotees. What is his name but that by which they refer to him out of love? It should come as no surprise, therefore, when we hear that Kṛṣṇa *nāma* is invested with Kṛṣṇa *śakti*, for Kṛṣṇa is completely invested in his devotees, causing them to address him affectionately. This is the Vedānta of Śrī Kṛṣṇa Caitanya: the supreme energetic (*śaktimān*) is simultaneously one and different from his energy (*śakti*), *acintya-bhedābheda-tattva*.

What is in a name? Everything. We are advised to be careful not to give out our name—nowadays our social security number—lest our identity be stolen. If we are present to this extent in our material name, how much more is Kṛṣṇa present in his name? Those names that are filled with his personal *śakti* often tell us more about him than he himself is aware of, for they speak of Kṛṣṇa as he is experienced by his devotees. Nothing is more endearing to Kṛṣṇa than hearing these names because they are expressions of his devotees' love for him.

As Gaura Kṛṣṇa continues to glorify *nāma-saṅkīrtana*, he speaks about the ease with which it is performed. It can be done at any time, in any place. Mahāprabhu explained this glory of *nāma-saṅkīrtana* to Rāma Rāya and Svarūpa Dāmodara: "There are no rules governing time or circumstance; even by chanting the name while eating or sleeping one can attain perfection."[5]

Although Mahāprabhu is talking about the ease of performing *nāma-saṅkīrtana* in this second verse of *Śikṣāṣṭakam*, it is worth noting that he uses the word *smaraṇe*, indicating *nāma-smaraṇam* as well. *Japa* of Kṛṣṇa *nāma*, wherein the holy name of Kṛṣṇa is whispered or remembered within the mind while counting on one's *japa-mālā*, is considered to be *nāma-smaraṇam*, as opposed to *nāma-kīrtana*. This meditation on Kṛṣṇa *nāma*, like *nāma-saṅkīrtana*, is not dependent on particular conditions to be fruitful. Unlike meditation in the *yoga-mārga*, which must be done under certain conditions and requires a pure heart for it to be fruitful, meditation on Kṛṣṇa *nāma* can be executed while walking or sitting and at any time, whether one's heart is pure or impure. Because the spiritual discipline of Kṛṣṇa *nāma* is ultimately an expression of the highest love transcending religious decorum, it is not bound by the regulations governing other spiritual disciplines, such as *yoga* and *jñāna*.

By comparison, the *jñāna-mārga* is not easy to tread. It emphasizes renunciation of the world (*sannyāsa*), the study of Vedānta, and introspection, all of which are difficult in comparison to *nāma-saṅkīrtana*. Although Mahāprabhu accepted *sannyāsa*, he did not tread the *jñāna-mārga*, and thus he was not preoccupied with the study of Vedānta and a life of introspection. Indeed, Śrī Īśvara Purī, Mahāprabhu's *dīkṣā* guru, advised him *not*

-to occupy himself with the typical duties of the *sannyāsa* order, such as the study of Vedānta. By calling Gaura a fool and telling him that he was not qualified to study Vedānta, Śrī Īśvara Purī revealed that in Kali-yuga people are not eligible for such practices. The study of Vedānta is a long and tedious undertaking, and in Kali-yuga time is short and memory poor. Instead of study, the simple practice of *nāma-saṅkīrtana* is mandated.

The ease and simplicity with which *nāma-saṅkīrtana* is performed does not diminish its value. On the strength of his experience of *nāma-saṅkīrtana*, Mahāprabhu converted many *sannyāsis* in Benares from the study of Vedānta (*jñāna-mārga*) to *bhakti-mārga*. At first these *sannyāsis* thought that Śrī Kṛṣṇa Caitanya was merely a sentimentalist and that singing and dancing were inappropriate for a *sannyāsi*, who is to be ruled by reason and scripture rather than mind and emotion. However, Mahāprabhu demonstrated that spiritual love, unlike material love, is grounded in knowledge, Vedānta. Indeed, Mahāprabhu made it clear that the simple expression of love that is at the heart of *nāma-saṅkīrtana* is the essence of Vedānta.

Thus when Mahāprabhu tells us in this verse of *Śikṣāṣṭakam* that *nāma-saṅkīrtana* is easy to perform and not encumbered by the rule of Vedic law, we should not think that it has no connection with Vedānta, that it is merely sentiment with no foundation in knowledge. Indeed, Kṛṣṇa *nāma* is both Brahman and the means to realize Brahman. Because Brahman is the exclusive subject of *Vedānta-sūtra*, the *Śikṣāṣṭakam*, being a commentary on the significance of Kṛṣṇa *nāma*, is also a commentary on the significance of Brahman and in this sense Mahāprabhu's commentary on Vedānta. Therefore, let us examine the essence of Vyāsa's *sutras* in light of Mahāprabhu's *Śikṣāṣṭakam* for the sake of adding further support to the idea that although Kṛṣṇa *saṅkīrtana* is easy to perform, it is nonetheless a practice that is well reasoned and scripturally based.

Vyāsa's *sūtras* begin by advising us to inquire into the nature of Brahman, *athāto brahma-jijñāsā*: "Now, therefore, is the time to inquire into the nature of the Absolute." Brahman, the *sūtras* tell us in the next of Vyāsa's aphorisms, is *janmādy asya yataḥ*, "That from whom the world emanates." Thus we are to inquire into the nature of the source of the world. How are we to make this inquiry? Vyāsa's third *sūtra* answers, *śāstra-yonitvāt*: "Revelation in the form of divine sound is the womb that gives birth to knowledge of Brahman." In pursuit of this mandate to seek revelation through revealed sound, one may encounter an obstacle: revealed sound is diverse and the *Vedas* a veritable jungle of sounds, apparently advocating many things. How can divine sound, which is diverse in its advocacy, give birth to the singular experience of Brahman? Certainly all paths do not lead to the same place. To this doubt *sūtra* 4 replies, *tat tu samanvayāt*: "When understood in context it is clear that the entirety of revealed sound is all pointing in the same direction." In other words, while there are many sound directives in scripture that appear to point in various directions, when the entirety of scripture is studied and its directives are understood in context, it becomes clear that scripture points to one thing: Brahman.

However, completing a comprehensive study of revealed scripture is no small undertaking and time in Kali-yuga is short.

Again, for these reasons Īśvara Purī advised Mahāprabhu not to study Vedānta. Instead, he advised him to chant one sound consisting of two syllables, "*kṛṣ-ṇa*." The most merciful Śrīla Rūpa Gosvāmī has written a similar statement: "The *śrutis*, the divine sounds of the *Upaniṣads*, like effulgent gems of knowledge are all casting light on one sound, 'Kṛṣṇa.'"[6] By this sound alone one can realize the nature of Brahman to a greater extent than one could through any other sound or through all other sounds combined. *Gopāla-tāpanī* reveals further that the Upaniṣadic statements cast light on the nature of Brahman, yet the sound "Kṛṣṇa" *is* Brahman, Param Brahman—*namo vedānta-vedyāya*[7]—and thus the *śruti* points to this sound for comprehensive knowledge of Brahman. Therefore, discussing Kṛṣṇa and chanting his name reveal much more about Brahman than that derived from uttering the Upaniṣadic dictums such as *tat tvam asi* and *so 'ham*. In this regard, Śrīman Mahāprabhu has said:

> The sounds of *śruti* remain far
> from the immortal nectar talk of Hari.
> Uttering them, there are no transformations of ecstasy,
> no hair standing on end, no trembling,
> no heart melting, no crying ecstatically.[8]

It is this ecstasy, which signals comprehensive knowledge of Brahman, that Śrī Caitanyadeva advocates in his *Śikṣāṣṭakam*. This comprehensive knowledge of Brahman is the experience of Brahman not merely as the source of the world but as *rasa*, sacred aesthetic rapture. Mahāprabhu's conviction that Brahman is *rasa* and that those who realize this are able to taste *rasa* is supported by *Taittirīya Upaniṣad*'s dictum *raso vai saḥ*, "Brahman himself is *rasa*. Attaining *rasa*, verily one becomes blissful."[9] When we understand that Brahman not only is the source of the world but also is sacred aesthetic rapture, we understand that *rasa* is the source of the world. The original *rasa* that Brahman is ultimately about—the love of Rādhā-Kṛṣṇa—is the source of the shadow of *rasa* that drives the world. The means to fully realize Brahman as *rasa* and thus transcend the mere shadow of *rasa* appearing as the world is to take shelter of sacred sound. Accordingly, the final statement of Vyāsa's *sūtras* declares, "Liberation through sound. Liberation through sound."[10] This *sūtra* ultimately refers to the most sacred sound of all—"Kṛṣṇa."

Mahāprabhu's understanding of Vedānta represented in his *Śikṣāṣṭakam* is also supported by *Śrīmad-Bhāgavatam*, which according to *Garuḍa Purāṇa* is Vyāsadeva's own commentary on the *sūtras*. As the *sūtras* conclude with an advocacy of *nāma-kīrtana*, so too does *Śrīmad-Bhāgavatam*. That ripened fruit of the tree of Vedic wisdom begins, in concert with *Vedānta-sūtra*, with the words *janmādy asya yataḥ*, which identify Kṛṣṇa as the source of the world. It comes to rest in the same way with a resounding advocacy of *nāma-saṅkīrtana*.[11]

Thus in this section we have examined the essence of Vyāsa's *sūtras* in light of Mahāprabhu's *Śikṣāṣṭakam*. We did so to add support to the idea that although Kṛṣṇa *saṅkīrtana* is easy to perform, it is nonetheless a practice that is well reasoned and scripturally based. As we have seen, while *nāma-saṅkīrtana* is easy to perform and anyone with faith in its efficacy can take it up, should one require a logical and scripturally based argument in favor of exclusive engagement in *nāma-saṅkīrtana*, the followers of Mahāprabhu's eightfold precepts can provide it.

Our discussion from the beginning of this chapter until now has centered on two virtues of Śrī Kṛṣṇa *saṅkīrtana*: the power inherent in Kṛṣṇa *nāma*, being filled as it is with Kṛṣṇa *śakti*, and the ease with which Śrī Kṛṣṇa *saṅkīrtana* can be performed. Consideration of these two virtues brought joy to Gaura Kṛṣṇa's heart. However, another thought suddenly plunged him into an ocean of despair. As he chanted the second half of this stanza of his *Śikṣāṣṭakam*, Śrī Kṛṣṇa Caitanya was overcome with lamentation followed by humility, and in the mood of a *sādhaka* he voiced a doubt.[12]

Mahāprabhu's doubt (*saṁśaya*) follows his original thesis (*viṣaya*). After stating his doubt, he strengthens it by citing evidence to support the antithesis (*pūrvapakṣa*) of his original thesis. In speaking in this way, Mahāprabhu follows the standard for discussion established in classical Vedānta commentaries, where *viṣaya*, *saṁśaya*, and *pūrvapakṣa* are invoked and then followed by *siddhānta*, or a conclusive, harmonizing synthesis that is supported by scripture. Let us examine Gaura's *viṣaya*, *saṁśaya*, and *pūrvapakṣa* and arrive at the *siddhānta*.

Mahāprabhu's thesis (*viṣaya*) is found in verse one and in the first half of verse two—Śrī Kṛṣṇa *saṅkīrtana* is the universal panacea. His doubt (*saṁśaya*) is found in the second half of verse two. There Gaura Kṛṣṇa says that he is unfortunate (*durdaivam*). This statement implies the doubt that while others may experience the wonderful effects of *nāma-saṅkīrtana*, this is not his experience. To strengthen this doubt with an opposing argument (*pūrvapakṣa*), Mahāprabhu offers evidence in the final line of his second verse. Therein he states that he has no love for Kṛṣṇa *nāma* (*nānurāgaḥ*), despite its merciful nature and the glorious effects said to accrue from engaging in it. Thus the antithesis is considered for the sake of the doubting *sādhaka*: perhaps *nāma-saṅkīrtana* is not the universal panacea after all.

The *siddhānta* that refutes the antithesis is that while *nāma-saṅkīrtana* is the universal panacea, to experience deep attachment for Kṛṣṇa *nāma*, one must approach it with the humility that Mahāprabhu expresses in this verse and verse three. Such humility implies a systematic approach under the guidance of Śrī Guru, for humility before Kṛṣṇa *nāma* involves humbling oneself before its bearer, through whom Kṛṣṇa *nāma* agrees to come into our lives. If anyone should doubt *nāma-saṅkīrtana*'s efficacy, not having experienced its effects even after engaging in it, such doubt should be set aside with the understanding that although Kṛṣṇa *nāma* can be chanted under any circumstances, to experience all of its glory one must approach Nāma Prabhu with the blessing of the *guru* and engage in *nāma-saṅkīrtana* under his or her guidance. In this way, gradually that which is impeding one from fully embracing Kṛṣṇa *nāma* will be removed, clearing one's path to spiritual progress. Thus *nāma-saṅkīrtana* comes to the world through the *guru-paramparā*, and Kṛṣṇa *nāma* chooses to reveal himself to those who honor this fact with all of its ramifications.

At this point one may justifiably question how a spiritual practice that is said to be unencumbered by restrictions of time, place, and so on—one that is relatively rule free—must be performed under the guidance of another, and all that this entails, for it to be effective. The answer to this doubt is that while *nāma-saṅkīrtana* transcends regulations governing other spiritual practices, there are nonetheless a number of things that help to create the conducive environment in which Kṛṣṇa *nāma* chooses to manifest its full glory. Śrī Kṛṣṇa himself corroborates this in *Bhagavad-gītā*. When describing the principal characteristics of *mahātmās*, he says that they are always engaged in *kīrtana* but then qualifies their participation in *kīrtana* with the words *yatantaś ca dṛḍha-vratāḥ*: "striving with determination in their observance of vows."[13] This unflinching observance of vows refers to following the guidance of Śrī Guru, *śāstra*, and *sādhu* in an effort to clear impediments and create a favorable environment for chanting.

What is it that impedes one's ability to take advantage of the glory of *nāma-saṅkīrtana*? It is misfortune (*durdaivam*) in the form of *anarthas*. *Anarthas* are literally "false values." They are those activities and thought patterns that get in the way of one's ability to understand that which is actually valuable. Under their influence one is distracted even while chanting Kṛṣṇa *nāma*, and on account of this one cannot take full advantage of the chanting.

Anarthas are varied and numerous. They arise from pious as well as impious acts within the realm of *karma*. They also arise from within the culture of Kṛṣṇa *bhakti*, for when as a result of Kṛṣṇa *bhakti* one develops good qualities, fame and fortune may also come. If one then mistakes these things for being worthy of cultivation, one tends to the weed as opposed to the *bhakti* creeper itself. Finally, *anarthas* also arise from offenses. Such sins of the soul are most detrimental. The root of all *anarthas*, however, lies in false pride, *pratiṣṭhā*. In this regard, Ṭhākura Bhaktivinoda cites the following verse from *Hari-bhakti-vilāsa* in his *Bhajana-rahasya*:

> After renouncing all *anarthas*,
> pride, their root, may still remain.
> One should avoid this *pratiṣṭhā*,
> as if it were sewage in one's drain.[14]

When *sādhakas* take to the path of *nāma-dharma* in humility with the blessing of Śrī Guru, they learn the method of *nāma-bhajana*. They learn what is favorable and unfavorable to the chanting. They show gratitude to the preceptor and, in doing so, become fit for spiritual practice, fortified by the wisdom, example, and grace of an experienced devotee. Adherence to the instructions of Śrī Guru thus equips *sādhakas* to progress despite *anarthas* in such a way as to gradually uproot them. Submission to the *guru* requires humility. Such humility fosters *bhakti*, and *bhakti* in turn fosters further humility.

Gaurahari speaks in this verse with lamentation as well as humility. He is lamenting his unfortunate condition and thus his heart swells up with *dainya*, humility. *Sādhakas* should feel like this. Such sincere humility attracts the grace and sympathy of Śrī Kṛṣṇa, thus terminating once and for all one's sorrowful sojourn of *saṁsāra*. Therefore Śrī Kṛṣṇadāsa Kavirāja Gosvāmī comments that although Mahāprabhu expresses lamentation in the second verse of *Śikṣāṣṭakam*, on hearing its significance all sorrow is silenced.[15]

Regardless of how fallen one may be, sincere acknowledgment of one's condition and subsequent humility attracts sympathy and thus power beyond oneself. Śrīman Mahāprabhu, the great master, teaches us this lesson here. One's unfortunate condition (*durdaivam*), when sincerely acknowledged and understood, begets a natural humility that attracts the sympathy of Kṛṣṇa *nāma* and thus a solution to the problem posed here in verse two that despite the glories of *nāma-saṅkīrtana*, one has no attraction for it. Humility and the desire to overcome *anarthas* do not cause all *anarthas* to immediately disappear, but because they attract the sympathy of Kṛṣṇa *nāma*, he stays with one despite one's background of offenses, and thus one is gradually purified by his grace and one's *nāma-bhajana* becomes steady.

তৃণাদপি সুনীচেন তরোরিব সহিষ্ণুনা ।
অমানিনা মানদেন কীর্তনীয়ঃ সদা হরিঃ ॥৩॥

tṛṇād api su-nīcena
taror iva sahiṣṇunā
amāninā mānadena
kīrtanīyaḥ sadā hariḥ

tṛṇāt api—like grass; *su-nīcena*—with humility; *taroḥ*—
than a tree; *iva*—like; *sahiṣṇunā*—tolerance; *amāninā*—
with modesty; *māna-dena*—with veneration; *kīrtanīyaḥ*—
to be glorified; *sadā*—constantly; *hariḥ*—Hari.

Being humble like a blade of grass,
being more tolerant than a tree,
expecting no admiration
yet showing others veneration,
one should glorify Hari constantly.

From the depths of his despair, Gaura Kṛṣṇa surfaced and touched the shore of hope, as he called out to his dear associates, "O Svarūpa, Rāma Rāya, listen to the characteristics of the kind of *nāma-kīrtana* by which *prema* awakens."[1] With these words Śrī Kṛṣṇa Caitanya prefaced his third verse of *Śikṣāṣṭakam*, his heart brimming with humility.

What kind of *nāma-kīrtana* awakens *prema*? Mahāprabhu says, "Constant chanting of Hari, humbly, tolerantly, and pridelessly." However poetic, this verse is often perceived as a bitter pill to swallow. There is a well-known saying in West Bengal, "When I heard about the *prema-dharma* of Śrī Kṛṣṇa Caitanya, I wanted to become his follower, but when I heard Gaura's third verse of *Śikṣāṣṭakam*, I knew it was impossible!" We should not think like this, for Kṛṣṇa *nāma* will gradually qualify us to chant with these symptoms as we progress from *aniṣṭhā bhajana-kriyā* through *anartha-nivṛtti* to *niṣṭhitā bhajana-kriyā*. Then, with steady practice uninterrupted by *anarthas*, our chanting will lead to *prema*.

That the path to *prema-prayojana* is paved with this verse of *Śikṣāṣṭakam* is shown in Mahāprabhu's dealings with Raghunātha Dāsa Gosvāmī, the *prayojana-tattvācārya* of Gauḍīya Vaiṣṇavism. *Prayojana-tattva* is literally "the metaphysical truth concerning the goal." The goal is *prema*, Rādhā *prema*, Kṛṣṇa *prema*. Because Raghunātha Dāsa discusses this ideal in depth in his writings, he has been dubbed the *ācārya* of the *prayojana* of Gaura's precepts. Earlier in his Jagannātha Purī *līlā*, Mahāprabhu personally placed Raghunātha Dāsa under the care of Svarūpa Dāmodara. At that time, Raghunātha Dāsa harbored a desire to hear something directly from the mouth of Mahāprabhu concerning the goal of life and how to attain it—*sādhana-sādhya-tattva*. When Svarūpa Dāmodara informed Śrī Caitanya about Raghunātha Dāsa's desire, Mahāprabhu smiled and stated that he had already appointed Svarūpa as Raghunātha's instructor because "he knows more than I do."[2] Then out of affection Gaura acquiesced and told the Raghu of Svarūpa the following:

> Do not listen to or speak gossip.
> Don't eat tasty food, nor be fashion conscious.
> Do not expect honor, yet honor others.
> Constantly chant Kṛṣṇa *nāma*,
> and mentally serve Rādhā-Kṛṣṇa in Vraja.
> These in brief are my instructions;
> from Svarūpa you will get specifics.[3]

After saying this, as if to sum up his instructions to Raghunātha Dāsa, Mahāprabhu uttered this third verse of *Śikṣāṣṭakam* to the *prayojana-tattvācārya*, making it clear that the path to *prema* runs through this verse of *Śikṣāṣṭakam*. In effect Mahāprabhu has said that if he were to distill all of his instructions on *sādhana-sādhya-tattva* into one verse, it would be this one! We might expect that the *prayojana-tattvācārya* would receive much higher esoteric instructions from Mahāprabhu than that which is emphasized in this verse: humility, tolerance, constant chanting, and so on. However, that Mahāprabhu spoke this verse only serves to underscore the importance of this fourfold mandate

on chanting. In speaking this verse to Raghunātha Dāsa, Mahāprabhu has in effect amplified it as if shouting it out publicly so
that all of his followers might rally around it. Just hear what the
most wise and holy poet Kavirāja Gosvāmī Śrī Kṛṣṇadāsa loudly announces in this regard:

Hands raised, I declare, "Listen all!
String this stanza on the thread of *nāma*
as a garland round your neck.[4]
Follow this *śloka* on the order of the Lord,
and surely Śrī Kṛṣṇa's feet will be your reward."[5]

Through the pen of Kṛṣṇadāsa Kavirāja Gosvāmī, we are further blessed with Mahāprabhu's own explanation of his poetry, in which he elaborates on the third stanza of *Śikṣāṣṭakam* to
Rāma Rāya and Svarūpa Dāmodara:

Although Vaiṣṇavas are advanced, they think themselves
to be lower than blades of grass and they tolerate everything like trees. As a tree is cut down, it does not protest,
and while dying in the heat, it does not request a drink. It
gives its wealth—its shade, and so on—to anyone who asks
while tolerating the heat and rain and simultaneously pro-
tecting others. Although Vaiṣṇavas are exalted, they are free
of pride nonetheless, offering everyone appropriate respect
and knowing that all *jīvas* rest within Kṛṣṇa. Aspiring in this
way, one who chants Kṛṣṇa's name attains shelter at his lotus feet and awakens *prema*.[6]

Singing Kṛṣṇa's name with this humble mentality, although essential for one in pursuit of *prema*, is no small accomplishment. As we have seen, one experiences this kind of chanting after attaining *niṣṭhitā bhajana-kriyā*, the short-term goal on the long and sometimes winding road homeward. From this point on, the road is straight but not narrow. It is broad and spacious, as rules become realizations and black and white turns to many shades of gray. This stage brings the heart of tender faith into harmony with the intellect. Thus one's faith becomes well thought out, and more, because this exercise fosters intensified *sādhana*, it results in inner certainty, firm faith derived from knowing beyond thinking. Furthermore, this spiritual confidence is followed by ever-increasing humility, as the *sādhaka* is humbled by the depth of the subject being explored. He or she now knows that all are students forever in this field, a field of knowing in which the knowledge itself has its own agenda that includes us. Suddenly the subject—the self—begins to perceive itself as an object in the hands of Kṛṣṇa *nāma*, and the world viewed previously through the limitations of the mind expresses its own life backed by the will of God.

The natural environment spoke to Mahāprabhu with friendly advice—be humble like grass and tolerant like a tree—and in the mood of a *sādhaka* he thought himself devoid of these virtues. Although it appears that nature does not speak to us in this way, it would be more accurate to say that we are not listening. Not only are we not listening to nature, whose every move is backed by God, we are not listening to Gaura. We are lacking in humility and tolerance, yet we never even think of

Gaura's verse when we walk on the grass and it bends humbly beneath our feet. We do not think of Mahāprabhu's poetry when the tree without complaint tolerates the summer sun to shade us. We must pay close attention to God and *guru*, to the book *Bhāgavata* and person *Bhāgavata*—*nityaṁ bhāgavata-sevayā*—if we expect them to share their secrets with us. *Niṣṭhā* involves the kind of attentive chanting that brings the world to life. As one's heart changes in *nāma-dharma* with the ongoing culture of humility and tolerance, one's surrounding environment that previously appeared to oppose one is perceived for what it really is—friendly. As the *sādhaka* realizes that he or she is surrounded by well-wishers, a sense of hope illumines the practitioner's heart.

The venerable Viśvanātha Cakravartī Ṭhākura explains in his *Mādhurya-Kādambinī* that the destruction of *anarthas* arising from good and bad *karma* is complete (*pūrṇa*) at the stage of *niṣṭhā*. However, Śrī Viśvanātha's term *pūrṇa* does not imply that *anarthas* are absolutely eradicated at *niṣṭhā*. As Viśvanātha Cakravartī Ṭhākura explains and *Śrīmad-Bhāgavatam* confirms, in this stage trace elements of these *anarthas* still remain, *naṣṭa-prāyeṣv abhadreṣu*.[7] Although the fire of material existence is practically extinguished (*bhava-mahā-dāvāgni-nirvāpaṇam*), the smoke has not entirely cleared. It will linger until one attains the stage of *āsakti*, at which time *anarthas* arising from one's *karma* are absolutely destroyed (*ātyantikī*) and liberation from material existence is complete.

As the *sādhaka* leaves the small world of the mind and its misery, he or she experiences the first characteristic of *śuddha-*

bhakti: freedom from suffering (*kleśaghnī*). Suffering is a result of *karma*, and it is experienced in the mind. What is happy for one is sad for another. One creature's funeral is another's festival. Beyond the relativity of the mind's perception of good and bad, happy and sad, is the realm of consciousness. In *niṣṭhitā bhajana-kriyā*, Kṛṣṇa *nāma* removes the mental blindfold and shaded glasses of ignorance (*tamas*) and passion (*rajas*) that have obscured the fact that we are of the nature of consciousness, not matter. In this stage one sees clearly (*sattva*), one's priorities are properly in place, and one is thus no longer deluded or distracted by false values, for knowing is the nature of *sattva*.

This passage from *aniṣṭhā bhajana-kriyā* through *anartha-nivṛtti* to *niṣṭhitā bhajana-kriyā* by the grace of Kṛṣṇa *nāma* is described by Śrī Sūta Gosvāmī in *Śrīmad-Bhāgavatam*:

> Kṛṣṇa, friend of the truthful devotee, certainly cleanses the heart of one who hears and chants about his virtuous activity. By constant service to the *bhāgavata*, impiety is all but destroyed and *naiṣṭhikī-bhakti* to the one who is praised with transcendental song is realized. At that time, the influence of *rajas* and *tamas*—lust and greed—no longer affect the devotee, who has become fixed in *sattva* and filled with happiness.[8]

"Constant service to the *bhāgavata*" refers to either hearing *Śrīmad-Bhāgavatam* or serving the person that personifies its precepts. If the result of regularly hearing the *bhāgavata* book and serving the *bhāgavata* devotee is the same, it should be clear that "hearing the book" involves much more than an intellectual exercise. Theoretical knowledge often fosters pride, whereas wisdom fosters humility. Nevertheless, one should study the *Bhāgavata* carefully. It gives a thorough bashing to the folly of mere intellectual exercise in the name of spiritual pursuit. It teaches one to use one's head, lowering it to soften one's heart. After all, it culminates in showcasing the softhearted, uneducated *gopīs'* unalloyed love for Vraja's cowherd prince. Constant chanting of Kṛṣṇa *nāma*—service without reservation—requires humility. These two go hand in hand.

Śrī Viśvanātha Cakravartī Ṭhākura writes of two kinds of *niṣṭhā*: one related to constant chanting, the other to humility and similar qualities. These two kinds of *niṣṭhā* are *sākṣāt bhakti-vartini*, *niṣṭhā* that is directly related to *bhakti*, and *tad-anukūla-vastu-vartini*, *niṣṭhā* that is related to that which is favorable to *bhakti*. Mahāprabhu's verse includes both of these. The words *kīrtanīyaḥ sadā hariḥ* indicate steadiness in hearing and chanting, and because these two are directly *bhakti*, *kīrtanīyaḥ sadā hariḥ* refers to *sākṣāt bhakti-vartini niṣṭhā*. The balance of the verse refers to *tad-anukūla-vastu-vartini niṣṭhā* because it refers to that which is favorable to *bhakti* but is not *bhakti* in and of itself, qualities such as tolerance and so forth.

Although humility is a quality favorable to *bhakti*, as opposed to being *bhakti* itself, among all favorable qualities it is unique in that in its fullest expression it comes very close to being *sākṣāt bhakti*. In his *Bṛhad-bhāgavatāmṛta* commentary, Śrī Sanātana Gosvāmī first describes humility as the essential devotional prerequisite. Ṭhākura Bhaktivinoda's *Jaiva-Dharma* has gone a step further, describing humility as an inherent character of Bhaktidevī herself. Later in his *Bṛhad-bhāgavatāmṛta*, Śrī Sanātana says as much.

As we have learned from exploring the second *śloka* of *Śikṣāṣṭakam*, Kṛṣṇa *nāma* is attracted to humility in the *sādhaka* and thus stays with him or her despite the continued presence of *anarthas*, including *nāma-aparādha*. The humility described in the commentary on the second verse, however, is not the full face of humility. It is the humility that removes obstacles to one's faith. This expression of humility makes one fit to receive the grace of God. It arises from the mind when one contrasts the mercy of Kṛṣṇa *nāma* with one's resistance to that mercy. The humility described here in the third verse of *Śikṣāṣṭakam*, however, comes from the soul.

Humility arising from the soul is a natural by-product of spiritual advancement. It begins to manifest at the stage of *niṣṭhā*. In *niṣṭhitā bhajana-kriyā* the finite soul approaches the door of the infinite. Above the door a sign reads, *kīrtanīyaḥ sadā hariḥ*: "Always chant the name of Hari," and the doormat to this threshold says, *su-nīcena*: "Be humble." At this junction between time and eternity—the finite and the infinite—a natural humility arises, as what it actually means to be finite is glimpsed for the first time. Here, finite is no longer a word but a realization, as is the humility it fosters. In his *Śikṣāṣṭakam* commentary, Ṭhākura Bhaktivinoda describes this condition as innate humility arising out of complete detachment from sense enjoyment. The humility of the second verse, in contrast, arises out of remorse for one's attachment for sense enjoyment.

Although *niṣṭhā* is an intermediate stage, that which we find in *niṣṭhā* is not inconsequential. Humility that appears in one who has something to be proud of is significant. The sense of humility attained in this stage carries the *sādhaka* into perfection and remains with him or her forever. Śrīman Mahāprabhu has highlighted the example of Śrī Rūpa and Sanātana Gosvāmīs for all *sādhakas* to take note of. After meeting them in Rāma-keli, Mahāprabhu spoke of their humility to his other associates. He said, "Seeing and hearing their humility, a stone would melt. Being pleased, I told them, 'Although you are exalted, you do not think yourselves so. Because of this, Kṛṣṇa will soon liberate you.'"[9]

As with humility, there are two standards of tolerance. The first type of tolerance is described in the *Gītā*. Śrī Kṛṣṇa tells Arjuna that he should tolerate material happiness and distress by understanding them for what they are. They are merely perceptions gathered by the senses, which the mind then deliberates on and determines to be good or bad, happy or sad, and so on. Our mind evaluates our experience as positive or negative and we live within the world of this mental determination. Rather than being tossed and turned by these mental calculations—avoiding the negative and pursuing the positive—we should cultivate tolerance within the context of spiritual practice, the fruit of which is experience of the nature of reality unfiltered by the mind. Such stoic, well-reasoned tolerance is an essential ingredient of basic spiritual practice.

Although this standard of tolerance is a tall order, Mahāprabhu's third verse speaks of an even loftier standard. It is a standard of tolerance that one attains through cultivating *nāma-saṅkīrtana*, one that begets *prema*. This standard of tolerance is described in *Śrīmad-Bhāgavatam*. Thus from the tolerance of the *Gītā* in the realm of intelligence, we move to the tolerance of the *Bhāgavata* in the realm of the soul:

> One who aspires for your mercy while tolerating the result of past misdeeds and offering obeisances with words, heart, and actions is the heir to *mukti* and eternal service at your lotus feet.[10]

This higher standard of tolerance begins with the end of one's principal *anarthas* that arise from *karma*. As this stage develops and one progresses to higher stages of *sādhana-bhakti* (*ruci* and *āsakti*), one's happiness and distress arise more from *bhakti* and *aparādha* than from *karma*. The lower standard of tolerance, in contrast, involves merely tolerating one's *karma*. The merciful Viśvanātha Cakravartī Ṭhākura discusses the higher standard of tolerance that begins with *niṣṭhā* and is fully realized in *āsakti* in his comments on the above *Bhāgavata* verse:

> The devotee thinks, "Since a devotee is not entirely under the rule of *karma* and time, that which appears to be their influence in my life is actually Kṛṣṇa's personal arrangement (to help me advance spiritually). Bhagavān certainly knows what is best for me, whereas left to myself I do not. Thus it is out of his mercy for me that Bhagavān personally involves himself in my life, sometimes giving me happiness

and sometimes giving me distress. He does this only in the course of engaging me in his service." One who thinks like this becomes the recipient (*dāya-bhāk*) of two results: liberation and divine service (*mukti-pada*).

The word *dāya-bhāk* implies inheritance. As an inheritance from a parent maintains a child, so the attainment of liberation and divine service maintain the life of the devotee. This inheritance is not given all at once. It comes in installments, beginning in *niṣṭhitā bhajana-kriyā*.[11]

Mahāprabhu's example of the tree also speaks loudly of *niṣṭhā*, for in addition to being tolerant, a tree is firm, deep-rooted, and immovable. *Niṣṭhā* means fixed, uninterrupted by the call of the mind and senses. Ironically, the first two symptoms of one who is fixed in the *sādhana* of *nāma-dharma*, humility and tolerance, involve considerable flexibility.

Bhaktivinoda Ṭhākura has explained that the tolerance mentioned in *Śikṣāṣṭakam* includes mercy. He has drawn this from Mahāprabhu's own explanation of the tree's tolerance. While tolerating the elements or when being cut down, the tree gives mercy to others. In his *Gītāvalī*, Bhaktivinoda Ṭhākura writes that when one becomes tolerant like a tree one will turn from violence and give protection to others. In his *Śrī Sanmodana-bhāṣyam*, he describes this quality of tolerance as pure compassion free from envy.

Although the qualities of humility and tolerance ornament the *sādhaka* and identify him or her as a *sādhu*, at the stage of *niṣṭhā* the *sādhaka* is free from egotism and thus is not attached to the respect that others offer. Such a serious *sādhaka* avoids the pride of being a *sādhu*. To avoid this respect, and because of seeing every living being as the resting place of God, a *naiṣṭhikī-bhakta* offers all respect to others in ways appropriate to their embodiment.

In concluding our discussion, it must be emphasized that this third verse of *Śikṣāṣṭakam* is about eligibility for attaining *prema*. While initial eligibility for treading the path of Kṛṣṇa *bhakti* involves only faith, because this verse is about firm faith—*niṣṭhā*—it speaks of further eligibility in the form of appropriate decorum and disposition. This further eligibility is in contrast to the word *durdaivam* in the previous verse, which indicates that one at the stage before *niṣṭhā* still has misbehavior based on false values. One's misfortune before *niṣṭhā* is that owing to this misbehavior one does not develop attachment to *nāma-saṅkīrtana*. Among all types of *anarthas* arising from this misbehavior, offenses to Kṛṣṇa *nāma* are the most damaging. Ṭhākura Bhaktivinoda writes in the eighth stanza of his poem *Śaraṇāgati*, "My *durdaiva* (misbehavior) is the ten offenses." Fortunately, these sins of the soul can be remedied by the attentive chanting that occurs at the stage of *niṣṭhā*—*kīrtanīyaḥ sadā hariḥ*—which clears one's path to *prema*.

Because the higher stages of *bhakti* cannot be attained without first coming to the stage of offenseless chanting, Mahāprabhu's followers have highlighted this verse and the stage of *niṣṭhā*, pointing to it as an interim goal to aspire for in pursuit of *prema*. Without *niṣṭhā*—without humility, tolerance, pridelessness, and attentive chanting—there will be no *prema*. The *naiṣṭhikī-bhakta*

exercises appropriate discrimination and thus clearly understands the difference between *kāma* and *prema*. Having left
kāma behind, he or she looks only forward with both eyes fixed
on the goal.

ন ধনং ন জনং ন সুন্দরীং কবিতাং বা জগদীশ কাময়ে ।
মম জন্মনি জন্মনীশ্বরে ভবতাদ্ভক্তিরহৈতুকী ত্বয়ি ॥৪॥

na dhanaṁ na janaṁ na sundarīṁ
kavitāṁ vā jagad-īśa kāmaye
mama janmani janmanīśvare
bhavatād bhaktir ahaitukī tvayi

na—not; *dhanam*—wealth; *na*—not; *janam*—followers;
na—not; *sundarīṁ kavitām*—beautiful women, wisdom,
verse; *vā*—or; *jagat-īśa*—O Lord of the universe; *kāmaye*—I
desire; *mama*—my; *janmani*—in birth; *janmani*—after birth;
īśvare—O Prāṇeśvara; *bhavatāt*—may there be; *bhaktiḥ*—
devotional service; *ahaitukī*—unalloyed; *tvayi*—unto you.

O Lord of the universe,
I don't want wealth, followers,
beautiful women, wisdom, or verse.
I ask only for unalloyed *bhakti* unto you,
O Prāṇeśvara, birth after birth.

The venerable Kṛṣṇadāsa Kavirāja Gosvāmī writes that after Mahāprabhu spoke the third verse of his *Śikṣāṣṭakam*, his humility grew and he prayed for pure devotion.[1] Gaura Kṛṣṇa's love increased his humility, and his humility increased his love. Kavirāja Mahāśaya comments that this is the nature of love: the devotee who has love feels that he or she doesn't have even a scent of it.[2]

After the heart is cleansed of the principal *anarthas* and *sādhana* becomes undeterred, the *sādhaka* develops a natural liking for *nāma-saṅkīrtana*. What was previously medicine now becomes food. Undeterred (*apratihatā*) devotion becomes unmotivated (*ahaitukī*) as well. This stage is known as *ruci* (taste), in which the *sādhaka* becomes attached to devotion itself unadulterated by fruitive desires or the desire for liberation. Thus the *sādhaka* has no interest in anything other than continued hearing and chanting in pure devotion, *śuddha-bhakti*. The *sādhaka*'s prayerful attitude begins to turn from submission in pursuit of spiritual emotion to an emotional life of spiritual longing.[3]

In this fourth verse Mahāprabhu describes *ruci* in terms of its *taṭastha-lakṣaṇa* (marginal characteristics) and *svarūpa-lakṣaṇa* (principal characteristics). Its *taṭastha-lakṣaṇa* is freedom from ulterior motive, and its *svarūpa-lakṣaṇa* is attachment to *bhakti*. Thus it is practically synonymous with *śuddha-bhakti* as defined by Śrīla Rūpa Gosvāmī.[4] Śrī Rūpa explains that *śuddha-bhakti* is characterized marginally as being unencumbered by desire for liberation, worldly achievement, or anything other than the pleasure of Kṛṣṇa. Its principal characteristic is a spirit of devotion favorable to Kṛṣṇa.[5]

Mahāprabhu describes *ruci-bhakti*'s marginal characteristics when he says that he has no desire for wealth (*na dhanam*). This means that he has no desire for economic development (*artha*) and by extension no desire for the wealth of religiosity (*dharma*).[6] When Mahāprabhu says he has no desire for followers (*na janam*), this includes attachment to husband or wife, children, friends, and the like, on which one spends one's money for sense enjoyment (*kāma*). Sense enjoyment is also underscored here by the word *sundarīm*, which literally means "beautiful" and thus represents the most formidable sense desire, the desire for companionship. As with *artha* and *dharma*, Mahāprabhu says he has no desire for *kāma* (*na janaṁ na sundarīm*). Nor does he have any desire for material knowledge or the arts (*kavitāṁ vā*). All this falls within the realm of *karma*. As Mahāprabhu has no interest in the realm of *karma*, similarly he has no interest in the knowledge that leads to liberation from this realm. The word *kavitām* in this verse can refer either to material knowledge or to knowledge that leads to liberation from material existence. The words *janmani janmani* refer to freedom from birth and death and therefore indicate *mokṣa*, or liberation.

Thus we find the four goals of humanity—*dharma*, *artha*, *kāma*, and *mokṣa*—represented in this verse. These four values, the so-called four *puruṣārthas*, or human (*puruṣa*) necessities/ideals (*artha*), include the entire range of human activities as well as transcendence of the human experience. Gaura Kṛṣṇa and the *sādhaka* who has attained the stage of *ruci* have no desire for any of them.

All human activities are rooted in desire, desire to attain pleasure and desire to avoid pain. Human desire can be divided into three categories: first, the desire for sense pleasure, which, while never satisfying one, nonetheless drives one to pursue the same sensual experience again and again; second, the desire for material acquisition, wealth, honor, power, security, and so on, which is progressive in that it does not mandate meaningless repetition but rather the drive to realize consistently greater goals; third, the desire for virtue, good character, righteousness, and so on, which is more progressive still and brings a sense of contentment and clear insight as to the nature of the world.

These three kinds of desires are products of the influence of the three *guṇas* of material nature—*tamas*, *rajas*, and *sattva*—manifesting in the human psyche. They are known, respectively, as *kāma* (pleasure), *artha* (power), and *dharma* (virtue). All three of these involve the perceived necessity to be something: to be gratified, to be powerful, to be virtuous.

The virtuous glimpse the fact that a life based on the perceived need to become something obscures the perception of that which we already are. This alone gives the virtuous life absolute value and superiority over aspirations for power and pleasure, which under the influence of virtue also have limited value. The truly virtuous ego is the potential bridge to transcendence of the false ego. Crossing that bridge with the energy of spiritual practice leads to *mokṣa*, freedom from necessity. Arriving there we find ourselves. We find that we have no need to *become* something because we already *are* something far greater than anything the limited human experience can afford. From the realm of the experienced (matter), we enter the realm of the experiencer (consciousness).

However, in this verse we find that Mahāprabhu's ideal transcends even *mokṣa*! Implicit in his lack of concern for transcending birth and death is the fact that for one who has attained *ruci* the web of *saṁsāra* is practically dismantled. It happened as a by-product of *nāma-saṅkīrtana*. The only desire that Mahāprabhu has at this point is the desire for *bhakti*, *bhakti* for its own sake—*bhavatād bhaktir ahaitukī tvayi*. Again, this is the principal characteristic of *ruci-bhakti*. With this in place, Mahāprabhu is now poised to taste all that liberated life includes—a transcendental relationship with God beyond the fetters of matter.

Matter provides only a distorted or false sense of pleasure/ joy, power/security, and virtue/wisdom. In connection with matter one can experience a temporal sense of sense pleasure, existence, and material knowledge. The pleasure, power, and virtue inherent in a unit of consciousness, a *jīva*, are far greater than that which one can experience in relation to matter. Dwelling in the self, one experiences the joy inherent in consciousness, nontemporal existence, and knowledge of oneself as a unit of consciousness. However, the inherent joy, security, and wisdom in the *jīva* are minute in comparison to the extent that these are inherent in God.

While security (*sat*), wisdom (*cit*), and pleasure (*ānanda*) are inherent in the *jīva* soul, God is the reservoir of these three. In God they are manifest to a much greater degree as *sandhinī*, *saṁvit*, and *hlādinī*. Thus the security, wisdom, and joy that the *jīva* who awakens to a loving relationship with God can experience are far greater than that which he or she can experience independent of such a relationship. When the liberated soul experiences liberated life in relation to God, it realizes its eternal form, eternal service, and the joy of love of God. This liberated life in relation to God is the ideal of *śuddha-bhakti*, which the *sādhaka* has been cultivating in the *sādhana* of *nāma-saṅkīrtana*. Before it manifests, one first becomes virtuous (*anartha-nivṛtti*). Virtuous life is followed by the initial phase of liberation from the influence of *karma* (*niṣṭhā*), and at the stage of *ruci* one begins to taste the ideal life of pure devotion in love of God. This taste appears in the form of attachment to hearing and chanting in *nāma-saṅkīrtana*, a special taste for postliberated life in comparison with which the four *puruṣārthas* pale.

In rejecting the four *puruṣārthas*, Mahāprabhu follows the lead of *Śrīmad-Bhāgavatam*. As mentioned earlier while discussing Mahāprabhu's first stanza, the *Bhāgavatam* picks up exactly where the *Bhagavad-gītā* leaves off. At the *Gītā*'s conclusion Śrī Kṛṣṇa says, *sarva-dharmān parityajya*: "Give up all concern with *dharma*."[7] This parallels the *Bhāgavatam*'s *vastu-nirdeśa-śloka*, which begins with the words *dharmaḥ projjhita-kaitavo 'tra*: "Rejecting all forms of cheating *dharma*."[8] By cheating *dharma*, this verse refers to all expressions of *dharma* not aimed at *prema*. Śrīdhara Svāmī, the ancient *Bhāgavatam* commentator who was so revered by Mahāprabhu, writes that the word *projjhita* (completely rejecting) in this verse includes foregoing not only *dharma* but *mokṣa* as well. Thus it should be clear from this important *Bhāgavatam* verse that the *Gītā*'s conclusion, which it follows in the wake of, is not merely the advocacy of transcending *dharma* in pursuit of liberation. As the *Bhāgavatam* points to *prema*, so too does the *Gītā*.

Kṛṣṇadāsa Kavirāja Gosvāmī cites the *vastu-nirdeśa-śloka* of the *Bhāgavatam* in his *Śrī Caitanya-caritāmṛta* in the context of explaining his own *namaskāra-śloka* glorifying Gaura-Nityānanda's divine dispensation of *nāma-saṅkīrtana*.[9] There he says:

> Kṛṣṇa and Balarāma, who previously played in Vraja,
> their splendor more magnificent
> than millions of suns and moons,
> have arisen in the east—the horizon of Gauḍa—
> out of empathy for the entire creation.
> The appearance of Śrī Kṛṣṇa Caitanya
> and Prabhu Nityānanda
> has filled the whole world with *ānanda*.
> As the sun and moon dissipate darkness
> and by their appearance illuminate all things,
> these two brothers preach *prema-dharma*
> and dispel darkness—ignorance covering living beings—
> with the gift of truth's substance, ultimate reality.
> I call the darkness of ignorance *kaitava*—cheating.
> It all begins with desire for *dharma*, *artha*, *kāma*,
> and *mokṣa*.[10]

In comparison to the light of love emanating from *prema*, the Vedic law concerning *dharma*, *artha*, *kama*, and *mokṣa* constitutes a dark cell for criminals. Gaura-Nityānanda's *prema-dharma*, drawn from *Śrīmad-Bhāgavatam*, comes to liberate every-one from the law of the sacred Vedic texts that came before it. Understood in terms of Mahāprabhu's *saṅkīrtana*, *Śrīmad-Bhāgavatam* is the New Testament of the Vedic scripture. All that has come before it that stresses the four *puruṣārthas* is superseded by its message of *prema*. Love of God—*prema-dharma*—fulfills all the laws and teachings of the Vedas. It is the *pañcama-puruṣārtha*, the fifth and ultimate necessity of hu-manity. As Mahāprabhu's merciful preceptor, Śrī Īśvara Purī, instructed him:

> While the fifth end
> is an ocean of immortal nectar—*prema*'s joy—
> the joy of *mokṣa* and the rest are but one drop at best.[11]

Thus we learn from Śrī Īśvara Purī that humans differ from an-imals not merely because they can reason but because by prop-erly exercising their reasoning they can truly love by learning to love God. Knowledge leads to detachment and *mokṣa*, but *prema*—love—leads to postliberated life. This is the message of the *Bhāgavatam* that Mahāprabhu embraced so closely to his heart. It is an invitation to participate in the eternal drama of Kṛṣṇa *līlā*.

As we have seen from this fourth verse of *Śikṣāṣṭakam*, Mahā-prabhu, representing a devotee who has attained *ruci*, stands well positioned to gradually experience *prema-dharma* and the drama of Kṛṣṇa *līlā*. When the *sādhaka* attains *ruci*, *śaraṇāgati* is fully in place, as his or her *śraddhā* has matured by virtue of being in touch with the land of faith. Now the stage—*saraṇāgati*—on which the drama of Kṛṣṇa *līlā* is performed is established in the *sādhaka*'s heart. The seeds of material desire are destroyed and the seed of *bhakti* that has already sprouted in the form of *śraddhā* begins to blossom.

The beauty of *śraddhā*'s blossom shines brightly, enchanted by the soothing moon of Śrī Kṛṣṇacandra. This blossom of *ruci* enchants the entire world and also charms the *sādhaka*'s heart. In its shadow stands material desire and the darkness it represents. As inauspiciousness is removed (*kleśaghnī*), the *sādhaka*'s life becomes truly auspicious (*śubhadā*). This auspiciousness begins at *niṣṭhā* and fully manifests in *ruci*. In his first stanza of *Śikṣāṣṭakam*, Mahāprabhu has referred to it and other effects of *ruci* with the words *śreyaḥ-kairava candrikā-vitaraṇam*. This phrase offers us further insight into the nature of the *ruci* that Mahāprabhu is describing here in verse four.

The word *śreyaḥ* means most auspicious, and here it refers to the fourfold auspiciousness that characterizes *śuddha-bhakti* in the stage of *ruci*. Śrī Rūpa describes this fourfold auspiciousness in his *Bhakti-rasāmṛta-sindhu*:

The wise say that from *bhakti*
fourfold auspiciousness arises:
natural ability to please all people
and attract everyone's affection,
possession of all good qualities,
and a condition of happiness.[12]

The *sādhaka* who has attained *ruci* is thus pleasing, popular, qualified, and happy. His or her happiness is neither material happiness nor the bliss of *brahmānanda*. It is the happiness of the prospect of *śuddha-bhakti*, which will grow within the *sādhaka* from this point to perfection.

Along with auspiciousness, three spiritual desires are experienced by the *sādhaka* at the stage of *ruci*. They manifest in the practitioner's intellect and are thus intentionally cultivated. These aspirations are the desire to serve Kṛṣṇa favorably (*ānukūlya-abhilāṣa*), the desire to attain a specific service to Kṛṣṇa (*prāpty-abhilāṣa*), and the desire to establish an affectionate relationship with Kṛṣṇa (*sauhārda-abhilāṣa*). They appear with greater intensity in the stage of *āsakti* and are fully established in the stage of *bhāva*.[13]

Thus *ruci* is the stage in which the *sādhaka* experiences tangible positive attainment. It is the beginning of actual love of God. The *sādhaka* has lost interest in material desire, and concern for liberation is obscured by the special taste for hearing and chanting that has awakened.[14] Such a *sādhaka*'s life is filled with auspiciousness and spiritual desire. The *sādhaka* starts to bid farewell to the world and its God (Paramātmā) from whom the *baddha-jīva* originates, as taste for Kṛṣṇa *līlā* begins to take precedence over Paramātmā's play of creation (*sṛṣṭi-līlā*) and all that it involves.

As Mahāprabhu turns from the world of material desire toward his inner ideal, he bows one last time to the manifestation of Kṛṣṇa that rules the world, referring to him in this verse by the name Jagadīśa. This name of God refers to the Paramātmā feature of God, the overseer of the world, and to the *aiśvarya* aspect of Mahāprabhu's Deity, Kṛṣṇa. Although it is not until the stage of *āsakti* that the Deity comes to sit in the *sādhaka*'s heart and fully displaces the Paramātmā, in the stage of *ruci* this displacement begins to manifest. Therefore, after addressing his Deity as Jagadīśa in the first half of this verse, Mahāprabhu then refers to him as Īśvara. By this name he refers not to Paramātmā but rather to his Prāṇeśvara, the Lord (*īśvara*) of his life (*prāṇa*), Śrī Kṛṣṇa. Thus he prays for unalloyed devotion to Kṛṣṇa, his Prāṇeśvara, life after life and not to the Paramātmā to whom he is bidding farewell.

Although the *baddha-jīvas* are originally manifest from the Paramātmā, if they are pursuing Vraja *prema*, they are focused on Kṛṣṇa, Rādhā-Kṛṣṇa.[15] However, Śrī Kṛṣṇa is lost in his Vraja *līlā* and forgetful of his Godhood. He is simultaneously God and forgetful of his Godhood, forgetful by the force of his devotees' love, which causes him to appear as an intimate friend or lover. Although it is true that despite Kṛṣṇa's being primarily lost in love he nonetheless retains his Godhood and can thus hear the prayers of his *sādhakas*, one can legitimately ask at what stage of spiritual practice a *sādhaka*'s prayers are capable of attracting Kṛṣṇa's personal attention and, furthermore, at what stage a *sādhaka*'s *sevā* becomes *līlā-sevā*, internal *sevā* that reaches Kṛṣṇa in his *nitya-līlā*.[16] While some may insist that Kṛṣṇa personally listens to the prayers of his *sādhakas* at any stage of *sādhana*, Ṭhākura Bhaktivinoda says, "The prayers of one who is a *śaraṇāgata* are heard by Śrī Nanda-kumāra."[17] As we have already learned, *śaraṇāgati* is complete in the stage of *ruci*.

By invoking the name Īśvara/Prāṇeśvara in his fourth stanza in contrast to the name Jagadīśa, Mahāprabhu implies that the *sādhaka*'s shift toward actual *līlā-sevā* has its earliest beginning in *ruci*, as one moves from the jurisdiction of the Paramātmā to the jurisdiction of one's personal Deity situated in his eternal *līlā*. The deepest import of the word *candrikā*, moonbeams, found in the first verse of *Śikṣāṣṭakam*, is that the influence of the *svarūpa-śakti* begins to show itself ever so slightly at the stage of *ruci*, as Śrī Kṛṣṇacandra benedicts his devotee. The influence of the *svarūpa-śakti* develops further as *ruci* matures and turns into *āsakti*, and it is complete in *bhāva*.[18]

Should any *sādhaka* who has not yet attained *ruci* or *āsakti* despair at this conclusion that in the early stages of *sādhana* the Paramātmā is involved in one's life more than one's personal Deity, he or she can take solace in Mahāprabhu Viśvambhara himself, as well as in the most merciful Nityānanda. Although Mahāprabhu prays to Jagadīśa and his Prāṇeśvara in this verse, his followers should pray to him. He is Viśvambhara, the maintainer of the universe, and he is Kṛṣṇa himself, the source of all *avatāras*.[19] He is the *yugāvatāra* and he is lost in *mahābhāva*. Thus he is both our Jagadīśa and our Prāṇeśvara. With one hand he reaches out to the *baddha-jīva* with the *yuga-dharma* and with the other he reaches up to the highest point of Vraja *prema*, as he dances in *nāma-saṅkīrtana*. He is Kṛṣṇa himself yet present in the world for *sādhakas* in his *ācārya-līlā*, and as his other self, Śrī Nityānanda Prabhu, he is present that much more, with both hands stretched out to all materially conditioned souls. Ṭhākura Bhaktivinoda has emphasized that worship of Gaura-Nityānanda in *dāsya-bhakti* begets Vraja *prema*. Worship in Nadīyā, live in Vṛndāvana. Gaura-Nityānanda hear the prayers of their *sādhakas*, even those who have no *ruci*, and as their *sādhakas* attain *ruci*, Gaura-Nityānanda begin to crack open the door to service in Kṛṣṇa's eternal *līlā*.

With a view to better understand *ruci* and the *rāgānugā-bhakti* that Mahāprabhu points to in his *Śikṣāṣṭakam*, it will be useful to conclude the commentary on this verse with a brief discussion of the two kinds of *sādhakas* pursuing the ideal of *rāgānugā-bhakti*—Vraja *prema*. Śrī Jīva Gosvāmī divides *sādhakas* who are cultivating *rāgānugā-bhakti* into two categories, *ajāta-ruci sādhakas* (those who have not attained *ruci*) and *jāta-ruci sādhakas* (those who have attained *ruci*). *Ajāta-ruci rāgānugā-sādhakas* are inspired to cultivate *rāgānugā-bhakti* by the association of those who already have a taste for *rāga-bhakti*. Śrī Jīva describes the *ajāta-ruci sādhakas* thus:

> Those who have not achieved *ruci* may still engage in *rāgānugā-bhakti* simply due to association with a devotee who has this kind of attraction, but they should engage in such practice combined with *vaidhī-bhakti*....The meaning of mixed *rāgānugā* and *vaidhī* is that one externally practices *vaidhī-bhakti* by making it one with *rāgānugā* to the extent that one is able to do so.[20]

What does it mean to externally practice *vaidhī-bhakti* while making it one with *rāgānugā-bhakti* according to one's ability? It means to engage in the practices of *vaidhī-bhakti*, such as hearing and chanting in *nāma-saṅkīrtana*, with a view to attain a specific taste for *bhakti* that follows in the wake of the divine love exhibited by Śrī Kṛṣṇa's eternal associates in Vraja and, as one's internal life begins to manifest, to engage in Kṛṣṇa *līlā smaraṇam*.

According to Śrī Jīva Gosvāmī, both *ajāta-ruci sādhakas* and *jāta-ruci sādhakas* engage in *līlā smaraṇam*. *Ajāta-ruci sādhakas*, though meditating on Vṛndāvana *līlā* through their *guru*-given Kṛṣṇa *mantra*, lack three things: a sense of identity in Kṛṣṇa *līlā*, a specific intention or goal concerning participation in the *līlā*, and the sense that their practice is being accepted as *līlā-sevā*. *Jāta-ruci sādhakas* are more advanced, and due to having attained maturity in *ruci*, they have a budding sense of their spiritual identity, a service ideal, and the sense that their practice is approaching *līlā-sevā*.

Those with and without *ruci* are also described by Śrīla Rūpa Gosvāmī in his *Upadeśāmṛta*, verses 7 and 8.[21] In verse 7 Śrī Rūpa explains that just as one afflicted by jaundice cannot taste the sweetness of sugarcane, similarly one afflicted by ignorance cannot taste the sweetness of Kṛṣṇa *nāma*. However, sugarcane is the natural cure for jaundice, and thus when one is cured from jaundice by eating sugarcane, one can taste its inherent sweetness. Similarly, one cured of ignorance by chanting Kṛṣṇa *nāma* can taste the sweetness inherent in Kṛṣṇa's holy name. In verse 8 Śrī Rūpa prescribes the devotional activities suitable for those who have cured themselves of ignorance by following his advice in verse 7, those who are tasting the sweetness of Kṛṣṇa *nāma*. These devotees are *sādhakas* who have attained maturity in *ruci*. Śrī Rūpa writes:

> While living in Vraja and following its inhabitants, one who possesses inherent, spontaneous love should utilize all one's time in attentively exercising the tongue in chanting and the mind in remembering Kṛṣṇa's name, form, qualities, and pastimes, in this order. This is the essence of all advice.[22]

As Mahāprabhu has made clear in this fourth verse of *Śikṣāṣṭakam*, one burdened by desires for wealth, women/men, and even wisdom lacks qualification to actually live in Vraja and follow its inhabitants in every sense. We should desire to become residents of Vraja, but as this verse of *Śikṣāṣṭakam* instructs us, we should be clear on what it means to deserve such a blessing, such that our desire is realistic and thus inspires us to attend to the work at hand. Only when material desires are checked by spiritual intelligence is steady *sādhana* possible. This steady *sādhana* floods material desires such that they no longer have any possibility of fructifying, and thus one gradually develops a taste for *sādhana*. As this taste intensifies, it turns into spiritual attachment for the object of one's devotion. This is the stage of *āsakti*, to which Mahāprabhu next turns his attention in all humility.

অয়ি নন্দতনুজ কিঙ্করং পতিতং মাং বিষমে ভবাম্বুধৌ ।
কৃপয়া তব পাদপঙ্কজ-স্থিতধূলীসদৃশং বিচিন্তয় ॥৫॥

*ayi nanda-tanuja kiṅkaraṁ
patitaṁ māṁ viṣame bhavāmbudhau
kṛpayā tava pāda-paṅkaja-
sthita-dhūlī-sadṛśaṁ vicintaya*

ayi—O; *nanda-tanuja*—son of Nanda; *kiṅkaram*—minion;
patitam—fallen; *mām*—me; *viṣame*—frightful; *bhava-
ambudhau*—sea of worldly life (*māyā*); *kṛpayā*—please; *tava*—
your; *pāda-paṅkaja*—lotus feet; *sthita*—fixed; *dhūlī-sadṛśaṁ*—
like a particle of dust; *vicintaya*—consider.

O son of Nanda, I am your minion,
fallen into *māyā*'s frightful sea.
Please consider me
as a dust particle at your lotus feet.

Once again Gaura Kṛṣṇa begs in great humility, this time requesting the gift of eternal service, praying for a spiritual identity. In doing so he simultaneously speaks about the nature of one's material identity, a sense of existence determined by material conditions.[1] In this way he teaches us how the *sādhaka* at the stage of *āsakti* yearns to be established in his or her eternal identity, retiring the fleeting sense of identity—the material ego—derived from the influence of material nature.

Material nature is constantly in flux, such that it is practically impossible for one under her influence to catch one's balance. As we toss and turn on the waves of material existence, material conditions change and so too does our sense of identity. A daughter becomes a wife, then a mother, then a grandmother, and then in the next life perhaps a son, and so on. Our desires and attachments determine our sense of self. Indeed, we are our attachments—a father based on attachment to sons and daughters, a husband based on attachment to a wife. Our sense of "I" is derived from our sense of "my."

The ground beneath our feet is moving. Although it looks solid, it is liquid. Speaking to Rāma Rāya and Svarūpa Dāmodara, Mahāprabhu compares material life to being lost at sea in a storm, *patitaṁ māṁ viṣame bhavāmbudhau*. This is practically a hopeless condition, and one can only be saved by help beyond one's own effort. Thus Śrī Kṛṣṇa Caitanya appealed to Nandatanuja for mercy, *kṛpayā*. Advanced *sādhakas* pray like this.

Reflecting on this verse of *Śikṣāṣṭakam*, Ṭhākura Bhaktivinoda sings, *anādi karama-phale, paḍi' bhavārṇava jale*: "Due to the results of beginningless *karma*, I have fallen into the material ocean."[2] Fortunately, as unimaginably long as it may take, beginningless *karma* can come to an end. In the stage of *āsakti*, the lingering smoke of the fire of *saṁsāra* is dissipated once and for all. This is the final end of *karma*'s influence, which began to disappear in the stage of *niṣṭhā*.

Proportionate to the demise of one's illusory karmic identity under the jurisdiction of Kṛṣṇa's *māyā-śakti*, one is able to establish a spiritual identity in relation to Kṛṣṇa under the jurisdiction of his *svarūpa-śakti*. This spiritual identity surfaces in the stage of *āsakti*. The surfacing of one's spiritual identity is the realized fruit of *sambandha-jñāna*, which is received in seed at the time of *dīkṣā* through the transmission of the Kṛṣṇa *mantra* from *guru* to disciple. This *mantra* assists the *sādhaka* in the *sādhana* of *nāma-saṅkīrtana*.

When the *sādhaka* realizes the import of *dīkṣā* and his or her *sambandha-jñāna* is thus complete, two results follow. One's external practitioner's body, or *sādhaka-deha*, becomes spiritualized, and the *sādhaka*, having completed the course of *sādhana-bhakti*, becomes eligible to engage in *līlā-sevā* to Kṛṣṇa in an internal spiritual body. In other words, as *āsakti* matures, *nāma-saṅkīrtana* brings "the bride named knowledge," Kṛṣṇa's *svarūpa-śakti*, to life in the *sādhaka*'s heart—*vidyā-vadhū-jīvanam*. This awakening heralds the appearance of the *sādhaka*'s *siddha-deha*.

Regarding the *sādhaka-deha*, Śrīman Mahāprabhu told Sanātana Gosvāmī that a Vaiṣṇava's body should never be considered material but rather transcendental and full of spiritual bliss.[3] He explained that this spiritualization begins with *dīkṣā*, and that when the *sādhaka* realizes the import of *dīkṣā*, his or her *sādhaka-deha* is so spiritualized that it becomes worshipable by even Kṛṣṇa himself!

> At the time of *dīkṣā*, Kṛṣṇa makes one equal to himself.
> He makes one's body full of consciousness and joy
> and worships the feet of that spiritual body.[4]

These words of Mahāprabhu can be rendered into English with two slightly different meanings, the first of which, as we have seen, finds one's *sādhaka-deha* worshipable by Kṛṣṇa.[5] The second possible rendering is similar but not quite as emphatic in its glorification of the *sādhaka-deha*. This reading merely tells us that Kṛṣṇa makes the devotee's body spiritual like his own so that the devotee can engage in the service of his lotus feet, for Kṛṣṇa cannot be served with material senses.[6] Thus the *sādhaka* realizes a spiritualized *sādhaka-deha* on attaining the stage of *āsakti*.[7]

Regarding the internal *siddha-deha* that is glimpsed at *āsakti* and further cultivated in *bhāva-bhakti*, Ṭhākura Bhaktivinoda writes in his *Bhajana-rahasya*, "At this stage (*āsakti*) of cultivating *nāma-sādhana*, the aspirant prays for knowledge of his eternal spiritual identity and for service to Kṛṣṇa (in that identity)."[8] In the same book, the Ṭhākura writes about how the gradual development that leads to the awakening of one's *siddha-deha* is outlined in *Śikṣāṣṭakam*:

> One should next become mature in one's worship on the basis of the first four verses, before accepting one's spiritual

body with the fifth verse. With this verse, one begins to take shelter of Śrīmatī Rādhārāṇī's lotus feet in the *siddha-deha* and then make gradual progress. By the time one has reached the sixth verse, one's contaminations have pretty much disappeared and one therefore has the right to worship in one's *siddha-deha*. If anyone tries to meditate on his spiritual body without having this qualification, his intelligence will be turned upside down due to his lack of strength.[9]

Further evidence that the *sādhaka's siddha-deha* is glimpsed and ultimately realized as a result of *nāma-saṅkīrtana* is given by Śrī Kṛṣṇa in his speech to Uddhava:

> Just as a diseased eye treated with medicinal ointment will gradually see more clearly, similarly a conscious living entity—the seer—when purified by hearing and chanting about my virtues, will gradually be able to see more clearly the underlying reality.[10]

Commenting on this verse in his *Rāga-vartma-candrikā* (1.9), Śrī Viśvanātha Cakravartī Ṭhākura writes that when sacred greed for Vraja *bhakti* awakens within the *sādhaka's* heart, the *sādhaka's* path is illumined both externally by Śrī Guru and internally by the indwelling oversoul, the *antaryāmī*. The Ṭhākura explains that a *sādhaka* may receive instructions about cultivating an inner spiritual identity in one of three ways. The *sādhaka* may hear directly from the mouth of Śrī Guru, from a qualified *sādhu,* or from within, as the instructions manifest of their own accord in the heart that has been purified by practices such as *nāma-saṅkīrtana*. At the stage of *āsakti*, the *sādhaka* attains this purity, evidenced by his or her being freed from the enjoying spirit and established in a spirit of service.

Speaking of the serving ego that forms the basis of one's spiritual identity, Mahāprabhu told Sanātana Gosvāmī, *jīvera 'svarūpa' haya—kṛṣṇera 'nitya-dāsa'*: "The eternal *svarūpa* of the *jīva* is Kṛṣṇa *dāsa*, a servant of Kṛṣṇa."[11] A serving ego is the basis of all expressions of *bhakti-rasa*. Whether one experiences oneself as a servant, friend, elder, or lover of Kṛṣṇa, all of these experiences of sacred aesthetic rapture are expressions of service intensified to different degrees. This serving ego is the antithesis of the enjoying ego, an identity based on material attachment in a self-centered world of "I" and "my." Any position in the world of divine service—even that of a dust particle at Śrī Kṛṣṇa's lotus feet—is desirable in comparison to the highest position in material life, *pāda-paṅkaja-sthita-dhūlī-sadṛśaṁ vicintaya*. Unfortunately, most would prefer to reign in hell than to serve in heaven.

In this fifth verse, Mahāprabhu does not aspire for a specific position of eternal service—as a servant, friend, parent, or lover—but appropriately conceals his budding life of internal *bhajana*. As Narottama Ṭhākura Mahāśaya sings, *āpana bhajana-kathā nā kahiba jathā tathā*: "One should not reveal one's *bhajana* to others,"[12] and *rākha prema hṛdaye bhariyā*, "Keep your love hidden in your heart."[13] By keeping one's love within, the fire of love compresses and becomes more and more powerful, propelling one onward to *prema*.

86

It is clear, however, that Mahāprabhu desires one of the eternal sentiments of Vraja *prema* from the fact that he refers to his Prāṇeśvara as Vraja's Nanda-tanuja. In *āsakti* Mahāprabhu's object of love and attachment is the cowherd son of Nanda. Nonetheless, the way in which Mahāprabhu would like to serve his object of love—what specific sentiment of love he has become attached to—remains hidden.

Āsakti literally means attachment. In the stage of *ruci*, a *sādhaka* is more attached to *bhakti* itself than to the object of *bhakti*. In *āsakti* this balance shifts, as the object of the *sādhaka*'s *bhajana* takes his seat in the heart and the *sādhaka* thus becomes attached to him personally. Just as our material sense of identity is based on attachment to sense objects, in the stage of *āsakti*, as spiritual attachment for Śrī Kṛṣṇa awakens through *nāma-saṅkīrtana*, a *sādhaka*'s attachment forms the basis of his or her budding sense of identity as an eternal servitor in one of four loving sentiments.

Spiritual attachment arising out of *nāma-saṅkīrtana* gives rise to spontaneous meditation on Śrī Kṛṣṇa in the same way that a materially attached person spontaneously thinks of the object of his or her attachment. One's mind goes effortlessly to that which one is attached to. As a less advanced *sādhaka*'s mind is prone to spontaneously wander from a deliberate effort to think of Kṛṣṇa, similarly in *āsakti* a *sādhaka*'s mind wanders spontaneously to thoughts of Kṛṣṇa when discussing mundane topics. Such is the powerful effect of *nāma-saṅkīrtana*. It fosters a meditative state in which the *sādhaka* participates internally in *līlā-sevā* from the vantage point of his or her *siddha-deha*.

As we have seen, the spirit of one's *svarūpa*, regardless of the particular form it takes, is selfless service. In this verse of *Śikṣāṣṭakam*, Mahāprabhu identifies himself as a *kiṅkara*, a servant. The word *kiṅkara* is derived from the two words *kim* (what) and *karomi* (I do), and thus implies, "How can I serve you?" This is the only question one needs to ask of God and *guru*. When asked in earnest with a pure heart, the subsequent answer gradually manifests as one attains the stage of *āsakti* and glimpses one's eternal serving nature.

নয়নং গলদশ্রুধারয়া বদনং গদ্গদরুদ্ধয়া গিরা ।
পুলকৈর্নিচিতং বপুঃ কদা তব নামগ্রহণে ভবিষ্যতি ॥৬॥

nayanaṁ galad-aśru-dhārayā
vadanaṁ gadgada-ruddhayā girā
pulakair nicitaṁ vapuḥ kadā
tava nāma-grahaṇe bhaviṣyati

nayanam—the eyes; *galat-aśru-dhārayā*—by streams of tears running down; *vadanam*—mouth; *gadgada*—faltering; *ruddhayā*—choked up; *girā*—with words; *pulakaiḥ*—rising of the hairs; *nicitam*—covered; *vapuḥ*—the body; *kadā*—when; *tava*—your; *nāma-grahaṇe*—in chanting the name; *bhaviṣyati*—will be.

While chanting your holy name,
when will my eyes flood with streams of tears,
my words falter, my voice choke up,
and my hairs stand on end?

In this verse Śrī Gaurasundara speaks to Rāmānanda and Svarūpa with deep spiritual emotion, longing for *prema*. Kṛṣṇa does not grant *prema* to a devotee until his or her longing to attain it becomes very intense. This intense longing typically arises in *bhāva-bhakti*, which is difficult to achieve. Śrī Rūpa has explained that *bhāva* cannot be realized even by long periods of intense practice devoid of taste and attachment, and thus one must first pass step-by-step through all the lower stages of *sādhana-bhakti*. Furthermore, it cannot be attained by any other form of spiritual practice, such as *jñāna* or *yoga*. *Bhāva* is also dependent on Kṛṣṇa's mercy, and even after one comes to the stages of *ruci* and *āsakti*, Kṛṣṇa does not grant it easily, certainly not as easily as he grants *mukti* to practitioners of other spiritual disciplines. Indeed, *mukti*, which is the goal of *yoga* and *jñāna*, is insignificant in comparison to *bhāva*.[1]

In this verse Śrī Gaurasundara prays for the ecstatic transformations known as *sāttvika-bhāvas*, which are characteristic of *bhāva-bhakti*. *Sāttvika-bhāvas* are involuntary bodily transformations resulting from spiritual emotion, and they are eight in number: paralysis, tears, perspiration, change of color, fainting, horripilation, trembling, and stammering. These involuntary symptoms are common when they manifest as a result of material emotions, such as fear or sadness, but uncommon when they manifest as a result of singing the name of Kṛṣṇa in *saṅkīrtana*. Such an occurrence signals the beginning of a life of eternal spiritual emotion in which one's mind is saturated with *bhāva*.

When *bhāva* arrests the mind, the mind becomes illumined and spiritual emotion moves throughout the body on the vehicle of the life air (*prāṇa*). As the life air is transformed under *bhāva*'s influence, *bhāva* in turn excites the body and affects its elemental constituents: earth, water, fire, and air. Paralysis manifests from *bhāva*'s influence on the earth element, tears and perspiration from its influence on water, change of color from its influence on fire, and fainting from its influence on air. *Bhāva* also affects one's body independently of its elemental constituents, causing horripilation, trembling, and stammering. Following the lead of the *tantra-śāstra*, Ṭhākura Bhaktivinoda comments that three of these eight transformations—tears, horripilation, and stammering—along with the *anubhāvas* (deliberate bodily movements) of singing and dancing are particularly symptomatic of *bhāva-bhakti*.[2] Mahāprabhu prays for the day that these three will decorate his body as he sings and dances in *nāma-saṅkīrtana*.

Although these external symptoms signal *bhāva*, because they also sometimes appear in material circumstances, they are not clear indicators of the presence of *bhāva*, and their absence does not necessarily mean that one has not attained *bhāva*. *Bhāva-bhaktas* often keep such symptoms in check and experience them within.[3] Furthermore, *bhāva* is sometimes imitated, causing these symptoms to manifest artificially. About such imitation Śrī Rūpa remarks, "Sometimes tears and other *sāttvika-bhāvas* appear in someone who does not possess the prerequisite spiritual qualifications, in someone whose heart is by nature slippery and who has simply practiced making a show of these external manifestations."[4] There is also the possibility that these symptoms will appear from time to time in sincere devotees who have not yet attained *bhāva*. Such instances are examples of Harināma Prabhu's encouragement, as the holy name sometimes chooses to draw *sādhakas* into a semblance of *bhāva*. Thus we are faced with the problem of how to distinguish a genuine *bhāva-bhakta* from a common person, an imitator, or a fortunate *sādhaka* experiencing a temporary reflection of *bhāva* and, furthermore, how to identify a *bhāva-bhakta* when he or she is keeping ecstatic symptoms in check.

The solution to this problem lies in the fact that *bhāva* is a deep spiritual realization that brings about not only bodily transformations but a change of heart. This change of heart is permanent, difficult to imitate, and exclusive to those who have attained *bhāva*. It is observable in the form of nine character traits: forbearance, concern that time should not be wasted, detachment, absence of false prestige, hope, eagerness, taste for chanting the holy name, attachment to descriptions of the transcendental qualities of Bhagavān, and affection for those places where he resides.[5] Thus while the external symptoms of ecstasy that Mahāprabhu speaks of in this verse indicate the attainment of *bhāva*, they must be corroborated by the appearance of these nine character traits. Furthermore, if we observe a devotee who possesses these character traits but not the *sāttvika-bhāvas*, such a devotee should be considered to have attained *bhāva-bhakti* while keeping the overt manifestation of *sāttvika-bhāvas* in check and experiencing them internally.

Needless to say, Mahāprabhu's own display of *sāttvika-bhāvas* arose from a very tender heart softened by *bhāva* and so saturated with *prema* that the *sāttvika-bhāvas* could not be checked.

96

No one could possibly imitate the external signs of ecstasy exhibited by Śrī Kṛṣṇa Caitanya. Although in this verse Mahāprabhu prays for the three *sāttvika-bhāvas* that are prominent in *bhāva-bhakti*, he does so to teach us about *bhāva*. He himself simultaneously exhibited extreme forms of all eight *sāttvika-bhāvas* along with *anubhāvas* that are so rare that Śrī Rūpa has not commented on them.[6]

Śrī Kṛṣṇadasa Kavirāja Gosvāmī's description of Gaurasundara's dancing in *saṅkīrtana*—dancing that made Jagannātha's eyes open wide and stare in disbelief—is perhaps the best illustration of this extreme ecstasy.

When Prabhu jumped and danced he was wonderfully transformed, as all eight *sāttvika-bhāvas* simultaneously erupted in him. The hair on his body stood on end and his body appeared like a smooth silk *śimulī* tree with thorns. Seeing his teeth chattering, people feared his teeth would fall from his mouth. Blood poured like perspiration from his pores. Stammering, he called to Jagannātha, *"jaja gaga jaja gaga."* His eyes poured forth water like a fountain, drenching everyone on all sides. In view of everyone, his hue changed from golden to reddish brown to the color of a jasmine. Sometimes he was stunned, and sometimes he rolled on the ground. His limbs became hard like sticks of dry wood and did not move. Losing his breath, he fell to the ground, and seeing this the devotees lost their own life breath. Tears poured from his eyes, mucus ran from his nose, and foam poured from his mouth like streams of nectar falling from the moon.[7]

Such descriptions of Gaura's ecstasy are compelling. They are filled with spiritual power and promise that *bhāva-bhakti*, although rare, is nonetheless within reach by the virtue of *nāma-saṅkīrtana*.

Thus far we have discussed the rarity of *bhāva-bhakti* and the appearance of *sāttvika-bhāvas*. We have not discussed, however, exactly what *bhāva-bhakti* is. Nor have we discussed what the life of a *bhāva-bhakta* consists of, as we have done for the *sādhana-bhakta*, whose life we detailed through the various stages of *sādhana-bhakti* in our discussion of the previous verses of *Śikṣāṣṭakam*. Therefore, let us turn our attention to the nature of *bhāva* itself and the inner life that it gives rise to.

Bhāva-bhakti is principally characterized by the ingress of Śrī Kṛṣṇa's *svarūpa-śakti* into the heart of a *sādhaka*. While the ingress of *svarūpa-śakti* is slight in the stages of *ruci* and *āsakti*, when *āsakti* is mature, this ingress is substantial and specific in nature, turning the spiritual attachment of *āsakti* into the spiritual emotion of *bhāva*. This ingress situates the *bhāva-bhakta* beyond the influence of material nature on the ground of pure existence, *śuddha-sattva*. This firm, pure ground of being is also known as *sandhinī-śakti*, one of the three components of Kṛṣṇa's *svarūpa-śakti*. One's spiritual identity emerges from this ground of pure existence and is shaped by the other two components of the *svarūpa-śakti*, the *saṁvit* (cognitive) and *hlādinī* (ecstasy) *śaktis*. Śrī Rūpa refers to this influence with the words *śuddha-sattva-viśeṣātmā*, which indicate a special liberated status within spiritual existence in which one is fully competent to cultivate spiritual emotion. In this pure condition, arrived at by the grace and power of Kṛṣṇa's holy name, his *mantra*, and the able guidance of Śrī Guru, one is qualified to taste the pure name of Kṛṣṇa, in which his form, qualities, and *līlās* are all contained.

The marginal characteristic of *bhāva-bhakti* is the effect it has on the devotee's mind and body, making them one with itself in the way that an iron rod becomes one with fire when placed within it. While in the paths of *yoga* and *jñāna* one's mind ceases to function because of being in static trance, when one's mind becomes one with *bhāva* it retains the ability to experience variety, giving rise to meditation on the dynamic nature of Kṛṣṇa *līlā*.[8] When the practitioner's body becomes one with *bhāva*, it moves completely under the influence of Kṛṣṇa's *svarūpa-śakti*. The *sādhaka-deha* is a spiritualized material body, and although it may appear to undergo material transformation, it is spiritual in that it is filled with *svarūpa-śakti*. In this regard, Mahāprabhu told Sanātana Gosvāmī that Śrī Sanātana's body was filled with *saṁvit* and *hlādinī-śakti—cid-ānandamaya*.[9]

Śrīla Rūpa Gosvāmī explains the difference between *bhāva-bhakti* and *prema-bhakti* with the analogy of the sun and its rays. *Prema* is the sun of love of God, and *bhāva* is one of its rays, *prema-sūryāṁśu-sāmya-bhāk*. *Bhāva-bhakti* is distinct from *sādhana-bhakti* and *prema-bhakti*, but it contains elements of both.[10] It is constituted of *prema*, but being only a partial manifestation of *prema*, it must be cultivated through a particular *sādhana* to bear fruit. The internal *sādhana* of *bhāva-bhakti* is a spiritual practice (*abhidheya-tattva*) that is fully informed because it arises out of a mature conceptual orientation (*sambandha-*

tattva), arrived at through the completion of *sādhana-bhakti*. Thus it is competent to enable one to realize the ideal (*prayojana-tattva*) of *prema-bhakti*. This *bhāva-sādhana* involves cultivating the various ingredients of aesthetic rapture by identifying with a particular role model in Kṛṣṇa *līlā* with a view to taste *rasa* and experience *prema*. One does so by meditating on the eternal drama of Kṛṣṇa *līlā* from the vantage point of one's inner spiritual identity.[11] Initially this participation is vicarious and eventually firsthand.

This internal *sādhana* is energized by *nāma-saṅkīrtana*. Indeed, *nāma-saṅkīrtana* begets meditation on Kṛṣṇa *līlā*. In the words of the most merciful Bhaktisiddhānta Sarasvatī Ṭhākura, "By the power of *kīrtana*, meditation on one's *svarūpa* arises."[12] *Śrī Bṛhad-bhāgavatāmṛta* says as much when it tells us that real meditation is "the fruit of *nāma-saṅkīrtana*."[13] Meditation is only superior to *nāma-saṅkīrtana* when one's meditation is so deep that it turns into internal *nāma-saṅkīrtana*.[14] Furthermore, Kavirāja Kṛṣṇadāsa writes that love of Kṛṣṇa is eternally existing and manifests itself in the course of hearing and chanting in *nāma-saṅkīrtana* as one's consciousness becomes purified.[15] After all, Kṛṣṇa *nāma* is nondifferent from Kṛṣṇa himself, and thus all of his *līlās* are present within his name. When one is established in *śaraṇāgati* through *nāma-saṅkīrtana* with the help of the conceptual orientation to Kṛṣṇa *līlā* found within the Kṛṣṇa *mantra*, one's heart is pure and thus a suitable place for the pure name of Kṛṣṇa to begin to manifest. At that time, Kṛṣṇa *līlā* springs forth spontaneously from Kṛṣṇa *nāma,* enabling one to fully identify with the *līlā* in pursuit of *rasānanda*.

Although Śrī Gaurasundara mentions only *sāttvika-bhāvas* in this verse, all of the ingredients of *rasa* are implied. A brief discussion of these ingredients will be helpful in understanding the inner life of a *bhāva-bhakta*. The ingredients of *rasa* are fivefold: *sthāyi-bhāva, vibhāva, anubhāva, sāttvika-bhāva,* and *vyabhicārī-bhāva.* They are best understood in the context of viewing and participating in a drama, in this case the drama of Kṛṣṇa *līlā*.

One's *sthāyi-bhāva* is the dominant spiritual sentiment through which one desires to serve Kṛṣṇa in his eternal *līlā*. It is the basis of one's spiritual identity that has dawned through the *sādhana* of *nāma-saṅkīrtana* and Kṛṣṇa *mantra-dhyāna*. In *bhāva* one views the drama of Kṛṣṇa *līlā* through the lens of one's developing *sthāyi-bhāva,* identifying with a particular sentiment expressed by one of Kṛṣṇa's eternal associates who has become one's role model.[16]

Vibhāvas, which arouse and intensify one's *sthāyi-bhāva,* appear in two varieties: *ālambana-vibhāva* and *uddīpana-vibhāva*. There are two *ālambana-vibhāvas*: the object of love and the embodiment of love. In the *līlā* the object of love is Kṛṣṇa and the embodiment of that love is one of his eternal associates who relishes a particular sentiment, such as romantic love. The *uddīpana-vibhāvas* are the personal qualities and attributes of the object of love. *Uddīpana-vibhāvas* are such only because the *bhāva-bhakta* has already begun to awaken the *sthāyi-bhāva* that causes them to be experienced in this light. One who already has love for something will experience things in relation to it as further stimulus for that love.

While *vibhāvas* stimulate one's *sthāyi-bhāva*, *anubhāvas* and *sāttvika-bhāvas* are responses to this stimulation. *Anubhāvas* are deliberate bodily movements, such as coy smiling, singing, and dancing, and *sāttvika-bhāvas* are involuntary bodily movements, such as tears or fainting. The final ingredient of *rasa* is *vyabhicārī-bhāva*, a transitory expression of love such as anxiety, humility, or jubilation. *Vyabhicārī-bhāvas,* although similar to *sthāyi-bhāvas,* are not powerful enough to be dominant emotions.

An illustration of how *rasa* expresses itself in *līlā-smaraṇam* should help the reader to grasp this difficult subject. If the *sthāyi-bhāva* being cultivated is romantic love, the *bhāva-bhakta* sees Rādhā as the perfect role model. She is the embodiment of the love that the devotee aspires to experience, and Kṛṣṇa is the object of that love.[17] While meditating on the *līlā*, the *vibhāvas*, such as the sound of Kṛṣṇa's flute and the coming of spring, will excite Rādhā's love, her *sthāyi-bhāva*. Thus the *bhāva-bhakta* who is identifying with that love in meditation is similarly stimulated. If the *bhāva-bhakta*'s *sthāyi-bhāva* is deeply felt, then it will result in a physical indication of the sentiment of romantic love that Rādhā experiences, such as a coy smile or sidelong glance. Such a physical indicator is an *anubhāva*. Involuntary responses also manifest in the form of tears and other *sāttvika-bhāvas* in Rādhā's person. As they appear in Rādhā, they also appear in the devotee cultivating romantic love for Kṛṣṇa. Finally, as *vyabhicārī-bhāvas* (transitory emotions), such as despondency and jubilation, appear in Rādhā, they also appear in the meditative *bhāva-bhakta* envisioning the *līlā*. All of these *bhāvas* occurring together heighten one's *sthāyi-bhāva* such that it ascends to the point of *rasa*, the zenith of spiritual emotion in aesthetic rapture.

Śrīla Rūpa Gosvāmī has compared *sthāyi-bhāva*'s ascent to *rasa* to the rising of the ocean in a monsoon. Just as the ocean is the source of clouds, which then shower rain on it and increase its tide, similarly the awakening of one's *sthāyi-bhāva* gives rise to the other emotional ingredients that shower down on the ocean of one's *sthāyi-bhāva*, increasing its depth and issuing forth a tidal wave of *rasānanda*. When the *bhāva-bhakta* tastes *rasa*, his or her *bhāva-sādhana* is mature.

The *bhāva-bhakta* directly experiences Kṛṣṇa in the world of spiritual emotion, and thus the Deity, who for the most part in *sādhana-bhakti* was theoretical, appears bigger than life. Having left the world where feeling and emotion are generated by the mind and have no potential to acquaint one with *rasa*, the *bhāva-bhakta* is now absorbed in the world of actual emotions in close pursuit of *prema-rasa*. Śrī Rūpa writes that the bliss of *bhāva* knows no bounds, *ratir ānanda-rūpaiva*. Mahāprabhu has said as much in the first verse of *Śikṣāṣṭakam* when he spoke of how Śrī Kṛṣṇa *nāma-saṅkīrtana* drowns one in an ever-increasing ocean of ecstasy—*ānandāmbudhi-vardhanam*. Experiencing this in the company of Rāmānanda and Svarūpa, Śrī Gaura-kiśora prayed to Kṛṣṇa after uttering his sixth verse of *Śikṣāṣṭakam*. With his heart melting in *bhāva* he cried out to Kṛṣṇa in the mood of Rādhā, "Make me your maidservant, my wage the wealth of *prema*."[18]

সুচারিতং নিমেষেণ চক্ষুষা প্রাবৃষারিতম্ ।
শূন্যারিতং জগত্ সর্ব্বং গোবিন্দবিরহেণ মে ॥১৭॥

yugāyitaṁ nimeṣeṇa
cakṣuṣā prāvṛṣāyitam
śūnyāyitaṁ jagat sarvaṁ
govinda-viraheṇa me

yugāyitam—a millennium; *nimeṣeṇa*—a moment; *cakṣuṣā*—
eyes; *prāvṛṣāyitam*—monsoon; *śūnyāyitam*—empty; *jagat*—
world; *sarvam*—entire; *govinda-viraheṇa*—separation from
Govinda; *me*—my.

A moment has become a millennium,
my eyes a monsoon,
and the entire world is empty
in my separation from Govinda.

As Mahāprabhu was absorbed in *rasa*, feelings of separation from Kṛṣṇa erupted and he raved like a madman in anxiety, remorse, and humility.[1] His love intensified such that his *sthāyi-bhāva* reigned like an emperor over all other attendant *bhāvas*, tasting them, nourishing itself, and immersing him in an ocean of *bhakti-rasa*. Śrī Kavirāja Kṛṣṇadāsa uses the word *rasāntarāveśe* to describe Mahāprabhu's condition—internally absorbed in aesthetic rapture. In doing so he highlights how this verse signals the onset of Mahāprabhu's *prema*, for internal absorption in *rasa* indicates that one has attained *prema*. As we shall see, *prema* makes its initial appearance in the dark night of the soul's unbearable pain of love in separation.

It is difficult to describe the depth of the emotive experience of *prema*. In *Bṛhad-bhāgavatāmṛta*, Nārada, while attempting to explain the nature of Rādhā's love for Kṛṣṇa, concludes that *prema* cannot be fully described. However, if we look to Rādhā's dearmost, Śrī Rūpa, we find a wealth of words on this most esoteric subject. In the beginning of his *Bhakti-rasāmṛta-sindhu*, Śrī Caitanya's chosen spokesperson defines *prema* thus: "The wise say that *prema* is *bhāva* intensified. It softens the heart completely and fosters a sense of possessiveness."[2] *Prema's svarūpa-lakṣaṇa* is intensification of *bhāva*, which as we learned from the previous *Śikṣāṣṭakam* verse is but a ray of the sun of *prema*. The complete softening of the heart and awakening of the sense that "Kṛṣṇa is mine" are *prema's taṭastha-lakṣaṇa*.

Intensification of *bhāva* transports the devotee from being influenced by Kṛṣṇa's *svarūpa-śakti* to being entirely situated within it. This is known as *svarūpāveśa*, full absorption in one's inner spiritual identity, or *svarūpa-siddhi*, the perfection of identifying with one's *svarūpa*, wherein one experiences the highest happiness. Rūpa Gosvāmī writes that this happiness exceeds the happiness of Brahman realization just as an ocean exceeds a mere drop of water.[3] Higher than the eternal peace and quietude of *brahmānanda* is the *svarūpānanda* of Bhagavān, in which he takes pleasure in his own eternal perfection. Higher still is *svarūpa-śaktyānanda*, in which Bhagavān's devotees take pleasure in him. It is this happiness, brought about by the intensification of *bhāva*, that *prema-bhaktas* taste. Thus Śrī Rūpa refers to the happiness *prema* affords as *sāndrānanda-viśeṣātmā*, a condensation of happiness (*sāndrānanda*) experienced by one who is completely enveloped in Śrī Kṛṣṇa's *svarūpa-śakti* (*viśeṣātmā*).[4]

This extraordinary spiritual happiness is strengthened by *prema*'s power to completely charm Śrī Kṛṣṇa, *śrī-kṛṣṇākarṣiṇī*.[5] Only *prema* has this power to bring Kṛṣṇa under one's control. *Prema* is directed not to Kṛṣṇa alone but to Kṛṣṇa along with his entourage. According to Śrī Jīva Gosvāmī, this is the significance of the word *śrī* in the phrase *śrī-kṛṣṇākarṣiṇī*. It refers to his entourage, which is constituted of his *svarūpa-śakti*. As *prema* captivates Kṛṣṇa, so too does it captivate his merciful associates. As it does so, it secures the *prema-bhaktas'* happiness in *svarūpa-śaktyānanda* or *sāndrānanda-viśeṣātmā*.

Thus with the intensification of *bhāva*, the *nāma-saṅkīrtana* that was previously a form of *sādhana* becomes the *sādhya*, as *bhāva* becomes *prema*—*prema-saṅkīrtana*. *Prema-saṅkīrtana* is not static but a dynamic, ongoing experience of ever-escalating love that flows like an ocean of nectar, sometimes retreating as the low tide of separation, causing waves of anxiety, and sometimes returning as the high tide of union, causing waves of jubilation.

Although love in separation is a theme that runs throughout Kṛṣṇa's Vraja *līlā*, it is highlighted in the case of Rādhā.[6] In his *Padyāvalī* compilation of verses, Śrī Rūpa has placed this seventh stanza of *Śikṣāṣṭakam* in the context of illustrating Rādhā's love in separation from Kṛṣṇa. In doing so Śrī Rūpa tells us that from this verse of *Śikṣāṣṭakam* we can understand that Gaura's *sthāyi-bhāva* is that of a lover—Rādhā's love for Kṛṣṇa. Thus after a six-verse preface, it is here in this verse that Kṛṣṇa as Gaura begins to actually confess his act of thievery. He tried to steal Rādhā's *bhāva*, and just see what difficulty it caused him!

Śrī Kṛṣṇadāsa Kavirāja Gosvāmī describes Gaura's *prema* in separation as being filled with anxiety (*udvega*), remorse (*viṣāda*), and humility (*dainya*). Anxiety is the second of ten conditions of separation experienced by all the inhabitants of Vraja. Thus it is not exclusive to romantic love, or *mādhurya-rasa*, although it is certainly heightened therein. Remorse is a *vyabhicārī-bhāva* that serves to augment one's *sthāyi-bhāva*. Humility can also be experienced as a *vyabhicārī-bhāva*, but to limit our discussion of it to this particular manifestation of humility will not do justice to its overall importance in relation to *prema-bhakti*. Śrī Sanātana Gosvāmī writes about the relationship between humility and *prema* in his *Bṛhad-bhāgavatāmṛta*:

Wise men define *dainya* as the state in which one always thinks oneself exceptionally incapable and low, even when endowed with all excellences. An intelligent person should carefully cultivate speech, behavior, and thinking that fix him in utter humility, and anything that stands in the way of it he should avoid. *Dainya* at its most exalted comes forth when *prema*, pure love of God, reaches full maturity, as it did in the women of Gokula when they were separated from Kṛṣṇa. When *dainya* fully matures, *prema* unfolds without limit. And so we see *dainya* and *prema* acting in a relationship in which each is both cause and effect.[7]

True spiritual humility is found in those well endowed with spiritual excellences, for the poor are humble only out of circumstance. There is no wealth greater than *prema*, and when we see humility in those who have it, we witness humility's full face. Mundane humility can be developed by human effort, but spiritual humility results only from receiving God's blessing. The *gopīs* exhibited this kind of humility in *viraha-bhāva*, or the ecstasy of love in separation. It is through feelings of love augmented by separation that this intense humility is experienced. Such humility is an integral component of *prema*, for just as humility fosters *prema*, *prema* in turn fosters humility.

Mahāprabhu's humility arises amid unbearable feelings of separation from Kṛṣṇa, as he begins to taste Rādhā's *prema*. This verse of *Śikṣāṣṭakam* represents Mahāprabhu's actual condition in Purī-dhāma during his *antya-līlā*, whereas all the previous verses are spoken in the mood of a *sādhaka* or *bhāva-bhakta* for the sake of teaching others. In his *antya-līlā* in Jagannātha Purī, Gaura Rāya has been called *vipralambha-mūrti*, "the form of love in separation," because he suffered so much in separation from Kṛṣṇa and thus taught the world about the inner life of *bhajana*. The merciful Bhaktisiddhānta Sarasvatī Ṭhākura writes in his *Vivṛtti* commentary on *Śikṣāṣṭakam* that the confidential secret of Gaurāṅga's *līlā* is that when Kṛṣṇa adopts the sentiment of a devotee as Gaurahari, he is situated in feelings of separation, *vipralambha*. Union (*sambhoga*) is achieved by first passing through separation. To demonstrate this, Śrī Kṛṣṇa manifests his eternal Gaura *svarūpa*, which is the incarnation of *vipralambha*.

Vipralambha is the love in separation that is exclusive to *mādhurya-rasa*. It expresses itself in four varieties: *pūrva-rāga*, *māna*, *prema-vaicittya*, and *pravāsa*. *Pūrva-rāga* is the separation lovers feel before they actually meet and formally acknowledge their love for one another. *Māna* is the separation that occurs when lovers quarrel with one another. *Prema-vaicittya* is the feeling of separation that occurs when lovers are in the presence of one another yet fear impending separation. *Pravāsa* is the separation that occurs when lovers are separated by distance and time. Commenting on the seventh verse of *Śikṣāṣṭakam* in his *Bhajana-rahasya*, Ṭhākura Bhaktivinoda writes that the sign of one's having attained the *sādhya* of *nāma-saṅkīrtana* is that one worships in the mood of separation. Similarly, *Śrī Bṛhad-bhāgavatāmṛta* states that the real sign of *prema* is that one performs *saṅkīrtana* in the agony of separation.[8]

Ṭhākura Bhaktivinoda emphasizes meditating on *līlās* involving *pūrva-rāga* or *pravāsa* in the cultivation of *prema*, as

Mahāprabhu does in this verse of *Śikṣāṣṭakam*. However, he also points out that devotees who have attained *prema* but have not yet left this world and taken birth in Kṛṣṇa's *prakaṭa-līlā* are only capable of fully experiencing *pūrva-rāga*.[9] The reason for this is that while *pūrva-rāga* can be experienced by hearing about Kṛṣṇa, seeing his picture, or visualizing him in meditation, the other three types of separation fully manifest only after having met Kṛṣṇa personally and having experienced the intensification of one's *sthāyi-bhāva* that takes place in Kṛṣṇa's *prakaṭa-līlā*.

Suffering from the pain of separation, Mahāprabhu assumed the mood of Rādhā and shared his feelings with Rāma Rāya and Svarūpa Dāmodara:

> In my suffering, the days seem to never pass. Each moment is as long as an age. Tears pour out of my eyes as though they were monsoon clouds. The three worlds have become void in Govinda's absence. I burn in the fire of separation, yet I cannot die.[10]

Although Rādhā's life in separation from Kṛṣṇa is unbearable, she cannot die because she knows that if she were to do so, it would cause Kṛṣṇa pain. Thus even though he has caused her the unbearable pain of separation, she remains selfless in her love for him. This is the secret of *prema*. Although Rādhā's love for Kṛṣṇa appears like the lust of a young girl for a young boy, the two are worlds apart. The basic difference between the two is that lust involves the desire to satisfy one's own senses, whereas *prema* involves the desire to satisfy Kṛṣṇa's senses.

In his *Gītāvalī*, Ṭhākura Bhaktivinoda beautifully expresses the spirit of Mahāprabhu's separation as experienced by one attaining *prema* through *nāma-saṅkīrtana*:

As I sang the names of the Lord, different *bhāvas* began to awaken within me. I saw Kṛṣṇa standing on the bank of the Yamunā, accompanied by the daughter of King Vṛṣabhānu. There he stood playing his flute under a *kadamba* tree, looking like a dancer about to go on stage. When I saw this divine couple, my mind became unsteady and I lost consciousness. I don't know how long it was, but when I came back to consciousness, I could not see them anymore. O *sakhī*! How can I go on living? A moment has become a millennium for me.

My eyes are streaming with tears like a downpour in the rainy season and the world has become a void. In Govinda's absence, my life airs no longer stay within me. Tell me how I can go on living. I have become so anxious. Still, taking shelter of *harināma* once again, Bhaktivinoda calls out to Rādhā's Lord: "Please show yourself to me. Please save me, or I will surely die."

Although the divine ocean of *prema* vacillates between the low tide of separation and the high tide of union, entrance into *prema* is only possible through love in separation. It is love in separation that enriches one's *sthāyi-bhāva* and thus makes one competent to fully participate in all aspects of Kṛṣṇa's Vraja *līlā*.[11]

This enrichment takes place after the *prema-bhakta* leaves this world and takes birth in Śrī Kṛṣṇa's *prakaṭa-līlā* in the association of the *nitya-siddha parikaras* of Rādhā and Kṛṣṇa. For both Rādhā's handmaidens and Kṛṣṇa's intimate friends who are involved in his romantic life, this development reaches the exalted state of *mahābhāva*. In this verse the words *yugāyitaṁ nimeṣeṇa* indicate *mahābhāva*. Because the exalted state of *mahābhāva* is the highest degree of intensification one's *sthāyi-bhāva* can reach, all that comes before it—*sneha, māna, praṇaya, rāga, anurāga*, and *bhāva*—is also implied in this verse. *Mahābhāva* is characterized, among other things, by its effect of making one feel a moment (*nimeṣa*) in separation to be like a millennium (*yuga*) and a millennium in union to be like a moment.

Śrīmad-Bhāgavatam describes *mahābhāva* thus:

No male or female in Vṛndāvana who tasted the festival of the eyes in the form of Kṛṣṇa's beautiful face, with its playful smile and cheeks adorned with dolphin-shaped earrings, was satisfied. Although they all felt happiness, it was mixed with frustration due to the momentary blinking of their eyes.[12]

Śrī Viśvanātha Cakravartī Ṭhākura comments:

This verse shows how, among the Vrajavāsīs, the *gopīs* and Kṛṣṇa's *priya-narma-sakhās* experience Kṛṣṇa's beauty most intensely….Unable to tolerate even the interruption that comes from blinking, they become angry. This is one of the signs of the highest love—*mahābhāva*—which is found only in the *gopīs* and nowhere else except perhaps in Kṛṣṇa's most intimate companions like Subala.[13]

In Gaura's separation, one moment—the blink of an eye—felt like a millennium. Such is the nature of distress. While joy passes all too soon, distress drags on as if forever. The word *yuga* means a millennium. In the grief of separation from Govinda (*govinda-viraha*), one moment turns into a millennium. However, *yuga* is also sometimes defined as "twelve years." Mahāprabhu spent the last twelve years of his *ācārya-līlā* in Jagannātha Purī experiencing Rādhā's love for Kṛṣṇa, her unbearable pain of separation, and in doing so he taught his followers how to taste this same love. The only hope for one whose heart is heavy in separation's grip is to pour forth a torrent of tears. Here Mahāprabhu compares his tears, which were comparatively slight in *bhāva-bhakti*, to a torrential downpour, *cakṣuṣā prāvṛṣāyitam*. In this condition he saw the world as vacant. Without Govinda the world held no charm for him.

What then is the value of Mahāprabhu's pain of separation? While on the outside the effects of *prema* appear like poison, on the inside they are filled with *ānanda*.[14] Although the ocean of Gaura's love caused him suffering in its low tide of separation, his love in separation on the shores of Jagannātha Purī made the ocean of love for Kṛṣṇa accessible to all. As he entered that ocean in low tide, so shall we—following his example through love in separation—and in so doing taste, as he did, the high tide of union discussed in the final stanza of *Śikṣāṣṭakam*.

আশ্লিষ্য বা পাদরতাং পিনষ্টু মাম্
অদর্শনান্মর্মহতাং করোতু বা ।
যথা তথা বা বিদধাতু লম্পটো
মৎপ্রাণনাথস্তু স এব নাপরঃ ॥৮॥

āśliṣya vā pāda-ratāṁ pinaṣṭu mām
adarśanān marma-hatāṁ karotu vā
yathā tathā vā vidadhātu lampaṭo
mat-prāṇa-nāthas tu sa eva nāparaḥ

āśliṣya—embrace; *vā*—or; *pāda-ratām*—devoted to his feet;
pinaṣṭu—break; *mām*—me; *adarśanāt*—hiding himself;
marma-hatām—torment; *karotu*—he may; *vā*—or; *yathā*
tathā—whatever he likes; *vā*—or; *vidadhātu*—let him do;
lampaṭaḥ—playboy; *mat-prāṇa-nāthaḥ*—Lord of my life; *tu*—
but; *saḥ*—he; *eva*—only; *na aparaḥ*—no other.

He may embrace me, devoted as I am to his feet,
or he may torment me and break my
heart by hiding from me.
Being a playboy, he is free to do whatever he likes,
for he alone is the Lord of my life.

In the previous verse of *Śikṣāṣṭakam*, Mahāprabhu tasted the ocean of Rādhā's *mahābhāva* in waves of separation from Kṛṣṇa. In this verse he tastes the high tide of Rādhā's *mahābhāva* in union with Kṛṣṇa. Love in separation (*vipralambha*) begets love in union (*sambhoga*). While separation is central to entering *prema*, its value is often considered to be the role it plays in enhancing loving union. Without separation, union cannot be fully experienced. As Ṭhākura Bhaktivinoda writes, "The pleasure felt in union cannot be properly appreciated without the experience of suffering in separation. That is the function of *vipralambha*."[1] Thus separation, while granting entry into Kṛṣṇa's *līlā*, also remains a permanent aspect of the drama of divine play, serving to enhance the desired union with Kṛṣṇa. Accordingly, even after embracing Rādhā, Kṛṣṇa may disappear and break her heart, only to reappear and embrace her once again.

Although separation and union complement one another, the highest reach of Rādhā's *mahābhāva* is experienced in union. Śrī Rūpa Gosvāmī calls this *mādanākhya-mahābhāva*. It is characterized by the ability to simultaneously taste many contradictory spiritual emotions in relation to Kṛṣṇa. *Mādanākhya-mahābhāva* is the exclusive experience of Rādhā, who as *mahābhāva-svarūpiṇī*, the personification of the highest love, experiences every facet of the brilliant blue sapphire-like Kṛṣṇa.[2] Indeed, she tastes love in ways that even he is unfamiliar with. The final verse of *Śikṣāṣṭakam* illustrates this love. Śrī Kṛṣṇadāsa Kavirāja Mahāśaya writes that it was originally spoken by Śrīmatī Rādhārāṇī.[3] As Gaura repeated Rādhā's verse, he tasted her *mahābhāva* and elaborated on it as if in conversation with his associates Rāma Rāya and Svarūpa Dāmodara in their Vraja *līlā* identities as Viśākhā and Lalitā.

Śrī Gaurahari's elucidation on his final verse of *Śikṣāṣṭakam* consists of thirteen simple *tripadi* Bengali verses. Both Gaura's verse and elaboration stress the underlying spirit of *mahābhāva* and only touch on the complexity of *mahābhāva*'s nuanced spiritual emotion. Thus, for the most part, Gaura spoke of the highest ideal in a way that the least qualified could take advantage of it. Let us try to do so.

Mahāprabhu's Bengali verses begin with the words *āmi— kṛṣṇa-pada-dāsī*, "I am a maidservant at the feet of Kṛṣṇa."[4] This statement is central to Mahāprabhu's entire elucidation because it reveals that Mahāprabhu has completed his *sādhana* of identifying with Rādhā's *prema*: he now completely identifies himself as a maidservant of Kṛṣṇa. This identification began in the fifth stanza of his *Śikṣāṣṭakam*, in which Mahāprabhu humbly prayed for divine service. On attaining his ideal, his humility has only increased. Such humility is one of the characteristics of Rādhā's *prema*, for although Rādhā is the Supreme Goddess, she conceives of herself as a mere maidservant. Although there is nothing greater than her love, it is nonetheless devoid of pride.[5]

Mahāprabhu's opening words also highlight the essential nature of Rādhā's love and that of love in general. Love is about service, about giving without concern for getting. The mystery of life is that while love involves selfless giving, it makes one whole. Śrī Rādhā is the best example of this in religious history.

Her love is selfless to the extreme, yet it makes her so whole, so complete, that God feels incomplete without her.

Mahāprabhu next says that he is a maidservant at the feet of one who "is the embodiment of transcendental joy and *rasa*," *tenho—rasa-sukha-rāśi*.[6] When we can identify the supreme enjoyer, we have the potential to give without reservation. Unconditional love requires that one condition be met: we identify the perfect object of love, the one who can absorb and reciprocate with our love unlimitedly, undeterred even by time. When we try to give selflessly to an imperfect object of love, we can only give so much, because an imperfect object of love is limited in its capacity to receive and reciprocate with our love. Although we do grow through such imperfect giving, the sense of wholeness we derive comes not as much from the imperfect object but from the perfect object of love, to whom we come closer through any act of giving and selflessness. As we know from the *Bhagavad-gītā*, it is the Absolute who is situated in sacrifice and thus realized through sacrificial acts.[7]

While sacrifice in any form brings us closer to the Absolute, sacrifice of one's own self endears us to God more than sacrifice of one's possessions. Above dutiful self-sacrifice lies complete self-forgetfulness in love. Such love is synonymous with the highest wisdom, on attaining which the absolute truth appears, revealing himself to be a lover. This is Rādhā's Kṛṣṇa, the perfect object of love, knowing whom nothing remains to be known.

When Mahāprabhu said that Kṛṣṇa is the personification of joy and *rasa*, he implied that any connection with him, either in divine union or separation, is joyful. However, Mahāprabhu goes on to explain another reason why Rādhā feels joy even in her separation from Kṛṣṇa: *sabe vāñchi tāṅra sukha, tāṅra sukha—āmāra tātparya*, "I only desire Kṛṣṇa's happiness. His happiness is the aim of my life."[8] Kṛṣṇa's happiness is what Rādhā lives for, thus if it makes Kṛṣṇa happy to ignore her, she is happy because she lives only for his pleasure. Her attitude pleases Kṛṣṇa so much that she realizes that he neglects her only to experience newer and newer nuances of her love for him.

If Rādhā is happy when Kṛṣṇa is happy, one may ask why Rādhā sometimes becomes jealous when Kṛṣṇa meets with another *gopī*. To answer this question, Gaurahari next explains the inner secret of Rādhā's outer display of jealousy (*māna*): *kāntā kṛṣṇe kare roṣa, kṛṣṇa pāya santoṣa*, "When a beloved *gopī* shows symptoms of anger toward Kṛṣṇa, Kṛṣṇa is very satisfied."[9] Although Rādhā sometimes appears jealous, her jealousy brings pleasure to Kṛṣṇa, who likes to taste her jealous love. She knows that he takes great pleasure in this *māna*, or apparent displeasure with him, but she also knows when to give in and accept his loving embrace once again. Śrī Kṛṣṇadāsa Kavirāja explains Rādhā's jealous love by saying that although her love is pure, it appears crooked.[10] He draws on Śrī Rūpa's explanation of *māna*: "love like a snake moves in a crooked way."[11] Sometimes Rādhā's *māna* is for apparent good reason (*sahetu*) and sometimes it is without cause (*nirhetu*). If it is without cause, it disappears of its own accord. If her *māna* is for good reason, Rādhā's hero must adopt appropriate means to pacify her, offering consoling words, gifts, and so on, all of which he delights in.

When Rādhā asserts herself, establishing her superiority and relishing Kṛṣṇa's embrace, some might conclude that her attitude is something other than that of a mere maidservant. Mahāprabhu, absorbed in her mood, responds to this charge: *mora sukha—sevane, kṛṣṇera sukha—saṅgame, ataeva deha deña dāna*, "My happiness is service. Kṛṣṇa's happiness is union with me. Therefore, I give my body to him in charity."[12] It should be understood that Rādhā acts assertively because she knows that in certain instances only she can satisfy Kṛṣṇa. Rādhā's delight in Kṛṣṇa's embrace is derived solely from the pleasure he draws from it. For Rādhā, union with Kṛṣṇa is not about her pleasure. Pleasure is merely a by-product of her service that she accepts only because doing so pleases Kṛṣṇa. For Rādhā, *sevā* is sweeter than *sambhoga*. Mahāprabhu therefore says, *kānta-sevā-sukha-pūra, saṅgama haite sumadhura*: "Service to Kṛṣṇa is the home of happiness. It is sweeter than union."[13] Thus despite Rādhā's outward forwardness, internally she maintains the mood of a maidservant, exemplifying selflessness to the extreme.

This selflessness is the ground on which *mahābhāva* dances, ground that even beginners can identify with as they set their sights on the towering ideal of the highest love. It is for this reason that Mahāprabhu emphasized Rādhā's selflessness in his final verse and subsequent elucidation. Rādhā's extreme selfless serving disposition establishes her as Kṛṣṇa's personal Deity, for in Mahāprabhu's ideal, love holds a position higher than God. Kṛṣṇa is God conquered by love, and Rādhā's love reigns supreme, such that Kṛṣṇa himself becomes her student. Rādhā's love is Kṛṣṇa's *guru, rādhikāra prema—guru, āmi—śiṣya naṭa*.[14]

This is the purport of *Śikṣāṣṭakam* revealed in its final *śloka*, echoing the essence of *Śrīmad-Bhāgavatam*'s *rāsa-pañcādhyāya*: love is its own reward.[15]

The love that Rādhā experiences, the *mādanākhya-mahā-bhāva* that she alone tastes, is such that Kṛṣṇa himself yearns to taste it. One may, however, justifiably question how Kṛṣṇa can lack anything. How can the Absolute be incomplete? The answer to this question can be found in the philosophy that underlies Kṛṣṇa *līlā*. Kṛṣṇa is full in himself, yet he is full of love, and love is never satisfied with itself. To taste himself more fully he manifests as two—Rādhā and Kṛṣṇa. As the *śruti* proclaims, *ekākī na ramate*: "Alone one finds no pleasure."[16] That which resides within Kṛṣṇa in an abstract sense as his inherent *hlādinī-śakti* manifests externally in a concrete form as Rādhā. These two, *rasa* and *prema*, are in essence one. Kṛṣṇa is *rasa* and Rādhā is *prema*. One has little meaning without the other. *Rasa* is the highest taste and *prema* is the means of tasting it.

Because the two, *rasa* and *prema*, are essentially one, Kṛṣṇa naturally desires to express this. He desires to be one with Rādhā, for as much as love requires two, it is all about two becoming one. However, he must do this in a dynamic sense to preserve his original purpose of fully tasting himself. He must become one with Rādhā while preserving both of their identities. This dynamic unity gives rise to Śrī Kṛṣṇa Caitanya, the combined form of Rādhā and Kṛṣṇa. He is both *rasarāja* and *mahābhāva*, *'rasa-rāja'*, *'mahābhāva'—dui eka rūpa*.[17] Kṛṣṇadāsa Kavirāja Gosvāmī describes this phenomenon:

Rādhā and Kṛṣṇa's love is a transformation of *hlādinī-śakti*. On earth, the one, Kṛṣṇa, has become two, Rādhā and Kṛṣṇa, eternally. Then, as Gaurasundara, these two formed a dynamic unity. *Praṇāma* to Gaura, who is endowed with Rādhā's countenance and personality.[18]

Although Kṛṣṇa is complete in himself, he is best equipped to taste love when he expands into two, Rādhā and Kṛṣṇa. Philosophically speaking, he does not lack anything; however, at that timeless moment when Kṛṣṇa becomes Rādhā and Kṛṣṇa, *līlā* is born and Kṛṣṇa loses himself in the drama of divine love. As Kṛṣṇa becomes absorbed in exchanges of love with his counterwhole, Śrīmatī Rādhārāṇī, he realizes that tasting love from her vantage point is more desirable than relishing it from his own. Consumed by his own play, he begins to ponder perhaps the greatest theological question: "How can I taste Rādhā's *prema*?"

Contrary to what one might expect, Rādhā is not inclined to give her *prema* to Kṛṣṇa, for she knows its power and how it will drive him mad. Furthermore, in her mind it would be improper to take a superior position to his, and in her supreme humility, she recoils at the thought that her superiority—the power of her love—might be broadcast all over the world. She knows that such a campaign would be a natural result of Kṛṣṇa becoming mad with her *prema* and losing his composure. Rādhā understands the far-reaching consequences of this. After all, while the secret of secrets is that Kṛṣṇa is her pupil in the school of love, outside of this private tutoring everyone else knows him as the Supreme Brahman, sought after by the most sober sages. He is God, to whom no one is superior.

Thus the necessity of stealing arises in Kṛṣṇa's mind. There is no other option. Kṛṣṇa concludes that he must steal Rādhā's *prema* if he is to taste it, and taste it he must, because he knows that it is superior to anything he has tasted. Whatever embarrassment stealing her love may bring as a consequence, Kṛṣṇa knows that true supremacy lies in tasting love—love is supreme. Furthermore, just as Rādhā wants to see him glorified, he wants to see her glorified. Despite his being a thief, he is the Supreme Truth. Truth be told, while most teach that God is the most worshipable object, Rādhā is the worshipable object of God. Thus Kṛṣṇa tries to steal Rādhā's *prema* to tell the world the truth. Although he is *pūrṇānanda-maya*, completely filled with joy, and *cin-maya pūrṇa-tattva*, the complete spiritual truth, the fact is that her love drives him mad.[19] Jaya Rādhe! Jaya Gaurahari!

Kṛṣṇa's madness, induced by Rādhā's *prema*, gives birth to Gaura *līlā* and Gaurahari's *prema-saṅkīrtana*, which in turn offers the world a golden opportunity. As we have learned, exactly what that opportunity is and the means to take advantage of it are explained in *Śikṣāṣṭakam*. After considering its significance, it is fair to ask if anything else remains significant in comparison. *Śrī Śikṣāṣṭakam* turns the religious world on its head. This poem has the power to awaken *yogīs* from trance and make them dance. As for *jñānīs* who have thought so much that their minds have stopped, *Śikṣāṣṭakam* tells them to think again, deeply.

Devotees, rejoice! Gaura composed the eight verses of *Śikṣāṣṭakam* for the purpose of advertising the purest love, and after composing them, Gaura tasted that love in *Śikṣāṣṭakam*'s final stanza and invited the entire world to do the same. *Śrī Śikṣāṣṭakam* should be recited daily and its deep meaning should be contemplated over and over again. These eight verses of Gaura Kṛṣṇa awaken *śraddhā* in the *sādhana* of *nāma-saṅkīrtana* and give *bhakti* in sequential steps culminating in Vraja *prema*. Blessed are those who take advantage of it. May they bless me by allowing me to follow in their footsteps.

VERSE ONE

1 *harṣe prabhu kahena,—"śuna svarūpa-rāma-rāya
nāma-saṅkīrtana—kalau parama upāya"* (CC. 3.20.8)

2 *kṛṣṇa-varṇaṁ tviṣākṛṣṇaṁ sāṅgopāṅgāstra-pārṣadam
yajñaiḥ saṅkīrtana-prāyair yajanti hi su-medhasaḥ* (ŚB. 11.5.32)

3 Sanātana Gosvāmī was the first to reveal how this verse refers to Śrī Caitanya.

4 BG. 18.66.

5 ŚB. 1.1.2.

6 *vācyo vācakam ity udeti bhavato nāma svarūpa-dvayaṁ
pūrvasmāt param eva hanta karuṇā tatrāpi jānīmahe
yas tasmin vihitāparādha-nivahaḥ prāṇī samantād bhaved
āsyenedam upāsya so 'pi hi sadānandāmbudhau majjati*
(*Śrī-kṛṣṇa-nāmāṣṭakam* 6)

7 *nāma-prema-mālā gāṅthi' parāila saṁsāre* (CC. 1.4.40)

8 *aiche prema, aiche nṛtya, aiche hari-dhvani kāhāṅ nāhi dekhi,
aiche kāhāṅ nāhi śuni* (CC. 2.11.96)

9 CC. 2.11.97.

10 *kṛṣṇa-nāma' pāraka hañā kare prema-dāna* (CC. 3.3.257)

11 *ādau śraddhā tataḥ sādhu-saṅgo 'tha bhajana-kriyā
tato 'nartha-nivṛttiḥ syāt tato niṣṭhā rucis tataḥ
athāsaktis tato bhāvas tataḥ premābhyudañcati
sādhakānām ayaṁ premṇaḥ prādurbhāve bhavet kramaḥ* (Brs. 1.4.15–16)

12 *Sādhu-saṅga* is also implied in the second verse of *Śikṣāṣṭakam*, as the spiritual practice discussed therein necessitates association with *sādhus*.

13 *Prārthanā* 4.2.

14 *Gopāla-tāpanī Upaniṣad* 1.5.

15 *sā vidyā tan-matir yayā* (ŚB. 4.29.49)

16 *yad icchasi paraṁ jñānaṁ jñānād yat paramaṁ padam
tad-ādareṇa rājendra kuru govinda-kīrtanam* (Hari-bhakti-vilāsa 11.441)

132

17 *prabhu tuṣṭa hañā sādhya-sādhana kahila nāma-saṅkīrtana kara,
—upadeśa kaila* (CC. 1.16.15)

18 *saṅkīrtana haite pāpa-saṁsāra-nāśana
citta-śuddhi, sarva-bhakti-sādhana-udgama
kṛṣṇa-premodgama, premāmṛta-āsvādana
kṛṣṇa-prāpti, sevāmṛta-samudre majjana* (CC. 3.20.13–14)

VERSE TWO

1 *aneka-lokera vāñchā—aneka-prakāra kṛpāte karila aneka-nāmera pracāra*
(CC. 3.20.17)

2 *ye yathā māṁ prapadyante tāṁs tathaiva bhajāmy aham
mama vartmānuvartante manuṣyāḥ pārtha sarvaśaḥ* (BG. 4.11)

3 *carācara-vyapāśrayas tu syāt tat-vyapadeśo 'bhāktas tad-bhāva-bhāvitvāt*
(*Vedānta-sūtra* 2.3.15)

4 Baladeva Vidyābhūṣaṇa appears to make this point in relation to Sanskrit.

5 *khāite śuite yathā tathā nāma laya kāla-deśa-niyama nāhi,
sarva siddhi haya* (CC. 3.20.18)

6 *nikhila-śruti-mauli-ratna-mālā dyuti-nīrājita-pāda-paṅkajānta*
(*Śrī-kṛṣṇa-nāmāṣṭakam* 1)

7 *Gopāla-tāpanī Upaniṣad* 1.1.

8 *śrutam apy aupaniṣadaṁ dūre hari kathāmṛtāt
yan na santi dravac-citta kampāśru-pulakādayaḥ* (*Bhakti-sandarbha* 69)

9 *raso vai saḥ rasam hy evayaṁ labdhvānandī bhavati*
(*Taittirīya Upaniṣad* 2.7.1)

10 *anāvṛttiḥ śabdāt, anāvṛttiḥ śabdāt* (*Vedānta-sūtra* 4.4.22)

11 *nāma-saṅkīrtanaṁ yasya sarva-pāpa praṇāśanam* (ŚB. 12.13.23)

12 *uṭhila viṣāda, dainya,—paḍe āpana-śloka* (CC. 3.20.15)

13 BG. 9.14.

14 *sarva-tyāge 'py aheyāyāḥ sarvān artha-bhuvaś ca te*

kūryuḥ pratiṣṭhāviṣṭhāyā yatnam asparśane varam
(*Hari-bhakti-vilāsa* 20.370)

15 *yāhāra artha śuni' saba yāya duḥkha-śoka* (CC. 3.20.15)

VERSE THREE

1 *ye-rūpe la-ile nāma prema upajaya tāhāra lakṣaṇa śuna, svarūpa-rāma-rāya*
(CC. 3.20.20)

2 *āmi tata nāhi jāni, iṅho yata jāne* (CC. 3.6.234). Svarūpa Dāmodara and
Rāmānanda Rāya both instruct Mahāprabhu in his effort to taste the
prema of Rādhā. They appear in Kṛṣṇa *līlā* as Lalitā and Viśākhā *gopīs*,
respectively. In that *līlā* they are the fast friends of Rādhā, and thus they
are well acquainted with her *prema*.

3 *grāmya-kathā nā śunibe, grāmya-vārtā nā kahibe*
bhāla nā khāibe āra bhāla nā paribe
amānī mānada hañā kṛṣṇa-nāma sadā la'be
vraje rādhā-kṛṣṇa-sevā mānase karibe
ei ta' saṅkṣepe āmi kailuṅ upadeśa
svarūpera ṭhāñi ihāra pāibe viśeṣa (CC. 3.6.236–238)

4 This verse may also be attributed to Mahāprabhu himself. In the context
in which it appears (CC. 1.17.32), it is ambiguous whether it is the final in-
struction of Mahāprabhu given to Śuklāmbara Brahmacārī or Kṛṣṇadāsa
Kavirāja Gosvāmī's comment on those instructions.

5 *ūrdhva-bāhu kari' kahoṅ, śuna, sarva-loka*
nāma-sūtre gāṅthi' para kaṇṭhe ei śloka
prabhu-ājñāya kara ei śloka ācaraṇa
avaśya pāibe tabe śrī-kṛṣṇa-caraṇa (CC. 1.17.32–33)

6 *uttama hañā āpanāke māne tṛṇādhama*
dui-prakāre sahiṣṇutā kare vṛkṣa-sama
vṛkṣa yena kāṭileha kichu nā bolaya
śukāñā maileha kāre pānī nā māgaya
yei ye māgaye, tāre deya āpana-dhana
gharma-vṛṣṭi sahe, ānera karaye rakṣaṇa
uttama hañā vaiṣṇava habe nirabhimāna

jīve sammāna dibe jāni' 'krṣṇa'-adhiṣṭhāna
ei-mata hañā yei krṣṇa-nāma laya
śrī-krṣṇa-caraṇe tāṅra prema upajaya (CC. 3.20.22–26)

7 ŚB. 1.2.18.

8 *śṛṇvatāṁ sva-kathāḥ krṣṇaḥ puṇya-śravaṇa-kīrtanaḥ*
hṛdy antaḥ stho hy abhadrāṇi vidhunoti suhṛt satām
naṣṭa-prāyeṣv abhadreṣu nityaṁ bhāgavata-sevayā
bhagavaty uttama-śloke bhaktir bhavati naiṣṭhikī
tadā rajas-tamo-bhāvāḥ kāma-lobhādayaś ca ye
ceta etair anāviddhaṁ sthitaṁ sattve prasīdati (ŚB. 1.2.17–19)

9 *tāṅra dainya dekhi' śuni' pāṣāṇa vidare*
āmi tuṣṭa hañā tabe kahiluṅ doṅhāre
uttama hañā hīna kari' mānaha āpanāre
acire karibe krṣṇa tomāra uddhāre (CC. 2.16.263–264)

10 *tat te 'nukampāṁ susamīkṣamāṇo bhuñjāna evātma-krtaṁ vipākam*
hṛd-vāg-vapurbhir vidadhan namas te jīveta yo mukti-pade sa dāya-bhāk
(ŚB. 10.14.8)

11 In *niṣṭhā* one may still have seeds of material enjoyment within one's
heart, but practice at this stage is so resolute that the seeds have no opportunity to fructify. One's *prārabdha-karma* may still play a small role as well,
but even such *karma* is edited by Krṣṇa. Thus one is substantially in the
hands of God.

VERSE FOUR

1 CC. 3.20.27.

2 CC. 3.20.28.

3 Śrī Jīva Gosvāmī divides prayer into prayers of submission (*samprārthana-*
mayī) and prayers of longing (*lālasāmayī*). He writes that prayers of submission belong to *sādhana-bhakti* and prayers of longing belong to
bhāva-bhakti. Although spiritual longing applies more to *bhāva-bhakti*
than to *sādhana-bhakti*, such prayers are not entirely inappropriate in
sādhana-bhakti, especially in the advanced stages of *ruci* and *āsakti*.

4 Ṭhākura Bhaktivinoda has also made this connection between the stage of *ruci* and attainment of *śuddha-bhakti*. In his *Bhakti-tattva-viveka*, the Ṭhākura identifies the devotee in the stage of *ruci* as one who has attained *śuddha-bhakti*, referring to such a devotee as an *uttama-adhikārī*. See the conclusion of *Bhakti-tattva-viveka*.

5 *anyābhilāṣitā-śūnyaṁ jñāna-karmādy-anāvṛtam*
   ānukūlyena kṛṣṇānu-śīlanaṁ bhaktir uttamā (Brs. 1.1.11)

6 Ṭhākura Bhaktivinoda includes the wealth of religiosity (*dharma*) within *dhana*.

7 BG. 18.66.

8 ŚB. 1.1.2.

9 CC. 1.1.2.

10 *vraje ye vihare pūrve kṛṣṇa-balarāma*
   koṭī-sūrya-candra jini doṅhāra nija-dhāma
   sei dui jagatere ha-iyā sadaya
   gauḍadeśe pūrva-śaile karilā udaya
   śrī-kṛṣṇa-caitanya āra prabhu nityānanda
   yāṅhāra prakāśe sarva jagat ānanda
   sūrya-candra hare yaiche saba andhakāra
   vastu prakāśiyā kare dharmera pracāra
   ei mata dui bhāi jīvera ajñāna-
   tamo-nāśa kari' kaila tattva-vastu-dāna
   ajñāna-tamera nāma kahiye 'kaitava'
   dharma-artha-kāma-mokṣa-vāñchā ādi saba (CC. 1.1.85–90)

11 *pañcama puruṣārtha—premānandāmṛta-sindhu*
   mokṣādi ānanda yāra nahe eka bindu (CC. 1.7.85)

12 *śubhāni prīṇanaṁ sarva-jagatām anuraktatā*
   sad-guṇāḥ sukham ity ādīny ākhyātāni manīṣibhiḥ (Brs. 1.1.27)

13 See Śrī Jīva Gosvāmī's commentary on Brs. 1.3.1 and 1.4.15–16.

14 There are two levels of taste in *ruci*, one dependent on certain conditions being in place (*vastu-vaiśiṣṭyāpekṣinī*) and one that is not dependent on any conditions (*vastu-vaiśiṣṭyanāpekṣinī*). For more on this, see *Mādhurya-Kādambinī*.

15 "Paramātmā" can refer to any of the three *puruṣāvatāras*. In this instance it refers to Mahā-Viṣṇu.

16 In *Rāga-vartma-candrikā*, Viśvanātha Cakravartī writes that Kṛṣṇa hears the prayers of his *rāgānuga-sādhakas* despite being lost in love, because although he becomes forgetful of his Godhood, he is still God. While his omniscience is suppressed by love, sometimes it surfaces.

17 *ṣaḍ-aṅga śaraṇāgati hoibe jāhāra, tāhāra prārthanā śune śrī-nanda-kumāra* (*Ṣaḍ-aṅgā Śaraṇāgati* 5)

18 Only as much as one is influenced by Kṛṣṇa's *svarūpa-śakti* is *nitya-līlā-sevā* possible. Kṛṣṇa takes pleasure only in himself. He is *ātmārāma*, or self-satisfied. His *svarūpa-śakti* manifests from within himself for the purpose of allowing him to taste himself. Thus his interaction with his *svarūpa-śakti* does not contradict his being *ātmārāma*.

19 The name Viśvambhara means "he who maintains the universe." Śrī Kṛṣṇadāsa Kavirāja explains that Gaura was named Viśvambhara at birth, but in his case the name refers to his nourishing the world through the gift of *prema*.

20 *Bhakti-sandarbha* 312.

21 Śrī Viśvanātha Cakravartī Ṭhākura has echoed Śrī Rūpa's seventh verse in his own discussion of *ruci* in *Mādhurya-Kādambinī*.

22 *tan-nāma-rūpa-caritādi-sukīrtanānu-*
smṛtyoḥ krameṇa rasanā-manasī niyojya
tiṣṭhan vraje tad-anurāgi janānugāmī
kālaṁ nayed akhilam ity upadeśa-sāram (*Upadeśāmṛta* 8)

VERSE FIVE

1 *ati-dainye punaḥ māge dāsya-bhakti-dāna āpanāre kare saṁsārī jīva-abhimāna* (CC. 3.20.31)

2 *Gītāvalī, Śikṣāṣṭakam* 5.

3 *prabhu kahe,—vaiṣṇava-deha 'prākṛta' kabhu naya*
'aprākṛta' deha bhaktera 'cid-ānanda-maya' (CC. 3.4.191)

4 *dīkṣā-kāle bhakta kare ātma-samarpaṇa*
  sei-kāle kṛṣṇa tāre kare ātma-sama
  sei deha kare tāra cid-ānanda-maya
  aprākṛta-dehe tāṅra caraṇa bhajaya (CC. 3.4.192–193)

5 See E. C. Dimock's edition of *Caitanya-caritāmṛta.*

6 Brs. 1.2.234.

7 In his commentary on ŚB. 10.29.10, Viśvanātha Cakravartī Ṭhākura writes
  that one's *sādhaka-deha* is completely spiritualized on attaining *prema.*

8 *Bhajana-rahasya* 5.

9 *cāri śloke kramaśaḥ bhajana pakva kara pañcama ślokete nija-siddha-deha vara*
  ei śloke siddha-dehe rādhā-padāśraya ārambha kariyā krame unnati udaya
  chaya śloka bhajite anartha dūre gela tabe jñāna siddha-dehe adhikāra haila
  adhikāra nā labhiyā siddha-deha bhāve viparyaya buddhi janme śaktira abhāve
  (*Bhajana-rahasya* 1)

10 *yathā yathātmā parimṛjyate 'sau*
   mat-puṇya-gāthā-śravaṇābhidhānaiḥ
   tathā tathā paśyati vastu sūkṣmaṁ
   cakṣur yathaivāñjana-samprayuktam (ŚB. 11.4.26)

11 CC. 2.20.108.

12 *Prema Bhakti-candrikā* 3.11.

13 *Prema Bhakti-candrikā* 9.19.

VERSE SIX

1 For more on *bhāva*'s rarity (*su-durlabhā*) and how it belittles *mukti* (*mokṣa-
  laghutākṛt*), see Brs. 1.1.33–37.

2 The *anubhāvas* of singing and dancing differ in *bhāva-bhakti* from the
  singing and dancing of *sādhana-bhakti* in that even though they are deliberate they are aroused by the ingress of *bhāva.*

3 See Viśvanātha Cakravartī Ṭhākura's commentary on ŚB. 2.2.2.

4 See Brs. 2.3.89. Here "slippery" refers to the veneer covering the heart of
  pseudo-devotees.

138

5 See Brs. 1.3.25–26.

6 In Brs. 2.2.12, Śrī Rūpa mentions swelling of the body and bleeding but does not discuss them because they are so rare.

7 *uddaṇḍa nṛtye prabhura adbhuta vikāra*
aṣṭa sāttvika bhāva udaya haya sama-kāla
māṁsa-vraṇa sama roma-vṛnda pulakita
śimulīra vṛkṣa yena kaṇṭaka-veṣṭita
eka eka dantera kampa dekhite lāge bhuya
loke jāne, danta saba khasiyā paḍaya
sarvāṅge prasveda chuṭe tāte raktodgama
'jaja gaga' 'jaja gaga'—gadgada-vacana
jalayantra-dhārā yaiche vahe aśru-jala
āśa-pāśe loka yata bhijila sakala
deha-kānti gaura-varṇa dekhiye aruṇa
kabhu kānti dekhi yena mallikā-puṣpa-sama
kabhu stambha, kabhu prabhu bhūmite loṭāya
śuṣka-kāṣṭha-sama pada-hasta nā calaya
kabhu bhūme paḍe, kabhu śvāsa haya hīna
yāhā dekhi' bhakta-gaṇera prāṇa haya kṣīṇa
kabhu netre nāsāya jala, mukhe paḍe phena
amṛtera dhārā candra-bimbe vahe yena
sei phena lañā śubhānanda kaila pāna
kṛṣṇa-prema-rasika teṅho mahā-bhāgyavān (CC. 2.13.101–110)

8 Brs. 1.3.10.

9 CC. 3.4.192. Notably, Sanātana Gosvāmī's body was infected with open sores and thus appeared to be subject to material conditions even though it was filled with *bhāva*.

10 Brs. 1.2.1. *Bhāva* is the goal of *sādhana*.

11 A semblance of this fully developed *bhāva-sādhana* is often performed prior to attaining *bhāva*, especially in the stages of *ruci* and *āsakti*. Indeed, Śrī Rūpa Gosvāmī mentions this *sādhana* involving an internal spiritual identity in his chapter on *sādhana-bhakti* in *Bhakti-rasāmṛta-sindhu*.

12 *kīrtana-prabhāve smaraṇa svabhāve se kāle bhajana-nirjana sambhava* (*Vaiṣṇava Ke* 19)

13 *Bṛhad-bhāgavatāmṛta* 2.3.165. Also see Sanātana Gosvāmī's commentary on *Bṛhad-bhāgavatāmṛta* 2.3.150, where he differentiates actual meditation from mere remembrance and states that true meditation on Bhagavān occurs in a mature stage of devotional development, wherein the soul (and not only the mind) comes in touch with God.

14 *Bṛhad-bhāgavatāmṛta* 2.3.151.

15 CC. 2.22.107.

16 In *bhāva-bhakti* one's *sthāyi-bhāva* requires cultivation to be fully experienced as one's eternal identity in Kṛṣṇa *līlā*. Jīva Gosvāmī has differentiated the *sthāyi-bhāva* that has not fully developed in *bhāva* from the fully developed *sthāyi-bhāva* of *prema-bhakti*. This development of one's *sthāyi-bhāva* involves the stages of *sneha* (affection), *māna* (jealous love), *praṇaya* (possessiveness), *rāga* (attachment), *anurāga* (subsequent attachment), *bhāva* (ecstasy), and *mahābhāva* (highest ecstasy) relative to the *sthāyi-bhāvas* of *dāsya* (servitude), *sakhya* (fraternal love), *vātsalya* (parental love), and *mādhurya* (romantic love). See *Ujjvala-nīlamaṇi*, "Sthāyi-bhāva-prakaraṇa" and also CC. 2.19.178 for details.

17 Typically in Gauḍīya Vaiṣṇavism devotees desire to become handmaidens of Rādhā and thereby experience her *bhāva* to an extent that would not be possible otherwise. In this case, Rādhā and Kṛṣṇa together become the object of love and Rādhā's handmaiden, Rūpa Mañjarī (Rūpa Gosvāmī), becomes the embodiment of love, the aspirant's role model. This is called *bhāvollāsa-rati* or *mañjarī-bhāva*.

18 *'dāsa' kari' vetana more deha prema-dhana* (CC. 3.20.37)

VERSE SEVEN

1 CC. 3.20.38.

2 *samyaṅ-masṛṇita-svānto*
  mamatvātiśayāṅkitaḥ
  bhāvaḥ sa eva sāndrātmā
  budhaiḥ premā nigadyate (Brs. 3.4.1)

3 Brs. 1.1.38.

4 Brs. 1.1.38.

140

5 Brs. 1.1.41.

6 All of the Vrajavāsīs experience love in union (*yoga*) and separation (*ayoga*). *Ayoga* is divided into *utkaṇṭhā* (anxiety) and *viyoga* (estrangement). *Viyoga* is further divided tenfold.

7 Sanātana Gosvāmī, *Śrī Bṛhad-bhāgavatāmṛta*, trans. Gopīparāṇadhana Dāsa (Los Angeles: Bhaktivedanta Book Trust, 2005), 2.5.222–25.

8 See *Bṛhad-bhāgavatāmṛta* 2.166–167.

9 Those cultivating *sakhya-rasa*, which is also prominent in Gauḍīya Vaiṣṇavism, experience the separation known as *ayoga* and the union known as *yoga*. *Utkaṇṭhā* is *sakhya-rasa*'s equivalent of *pūrva-rāga*. It means eagerness to meet Kṛṣṇa for the first time after having heard about him.

10 *udvege divasa nā yāya,*
   'kṣaṇa' haila 'yuga'-sama varṣāra megha-prāya aśru variṣe nayana
   govinda-virahe śūnya ha-ila tribhuvana tuṣānale poḍe, yena nā yāya jīvana
   (CC. 3.20.40–41)

11 The stages of enrichment are *sneha, māna, praṇaya, rāga, anurāga, bhāva,* and *mahābhāva*. The stage of *bhāva* here is different from the stage of *bhāva* preceding *prema-bhakti*. Furthermore, this stage of *bhāva* within *prema* is sometimes considered one with *mahābhāva* and thus is not mentioned. All of the basic *sthāyi-bhāvas* are enriched in *rāgānugā-bhakti*, but not all of them are enriched up to the stage of *mahābhāva*.

12 *yasyānanaṁ makara-kuṇḍala-cāru-karṇa-*
   bhrājat-kapola-subhagaṁ savilāsa-hāsam
   nityotsavaṁ na tatṛpur dṛśibhiḥ pibantyo
   nāryo narāś ca muditaḥ kupitā nimeś ca (ŚB. 9.24.65)

13 *Caitanya-caritāmṛta* 2.23.55 also confirms that Kṛṣṇa's most intimate friends experience *mahābhāva*, although not to the same extent that the handmaidens of Rādhā do. In this verse of *Caitanya-caritāmṛta*, the word *bhāva* means *mahābhāva*.

14 CC. 2.2.50.

VERSE EIGHT

1 *vinā vipralambhāśraya, sambhogera puṣṭi nāya, tai vipralambhera vidhāna* (*Gītā-mālā* 4.25.1)

2 Rādhā's handmaidens experience her love as well by way of complete identification with her *bhāva* in *rādhā-dāsyam*. Śrī Rūpa Gosvāmī calls this identification *tad-bhāvecchāmayī*. Mahāprabhu gave people of the world the opportunity to taste this through his dispensation of Śrī Kṛṣṇa *saṅkīrtana*.

3 CC. 3.20.33–36.

4 CC. 3.20.48.

5 CC. 1.4.129.

6 CC. 3.20.48.

7 BG. 3.15.

8 CC. 3.20.52.

9 CC. 3.20.54.

10 CC. 1.4.130.

11 *aher iva gatiḥ premṇaḥ svabhāva-kuṭilā bhavet*
ato hetor ahetoś ca yūnor māna udañcati (*Ujjvala-nīlamaṇi* 15.102)

12 CC. 3.20.59.

13 CC. 3.20.60.

14 CC. 1.4.124.

15 At the conclusion of these five chapters of the *Bhāgavata*, which represent its heart, Kṛṣṇa tells the *gopīs* that their love for him is its own reward. By their love they have completely purchased him and exhausted his capacity to reciprocate. Thus their love becomes the object of his veneration.

16 *Bṛhadāraṇyaka Upaniṣad* 1.4.3.

17 CC. 2.8.282.

18 *rādhā kṛṣṇa-praṇaya-vikṛtir hlādinī śaktir asmād
ekātmānāv api bhuvi purā deha-bhedaṁ gatau tau
caitanyākhyaṁ prakaṭam adhunā tad-dvayaṁ caikyam āptaṁ
rādhā-bhāva-dyuti-suvalitaṁ naumi kṛṣṇa-svarūpam* (CC. I.1.5)

19 CC. I.4.122.

ABHIDHEYA-TATTVA The means to attain spiritual perfection.

ĀCĀRYA-LĪLĀ God's pastime of appearing in the world to
teach about himself.

ACINTYA-BHEDĀBHEDA-TATTVA The inconceivable, simul-
taneous oneness and difference between God and his energy.

ADHIKĀRA The eligibility to perform a certain type of work.

ADHIKĀRĪ The possessor of eligibility.

ADVAYA-JÑĀNA-TATTVA The metaphysical truth about the
nondual nature of the Absolute.

AHAITUKĪ Without ulterior motive.

AHAṄKĀRA The material ego, characterized by the attitude of
"I" and "mine."

AIŚVARYA Majesty.

AJĀTA-RUCI Without taste. Refers to those whose spiritual
practice has not reached the stage of *ruci*.

AKHILA-RASĀMṚTA-MŪRTI The form of all varieties of
aesthetic rapture.

AMṚTA Immortality or nectar.

ĀNANDA Spiritual bliss.

ANARTHA False value. Refers to an obstacle to *bhakti* residing
within the practitioner's heart.

ANARTHA-NIVṚTTI A stage of *bhakti* in which the primary
obstacles to *bhakti* have been eradicated.

ANIṢṬHĀ BHAJANA-KRIYĀ Devotional practice that is not
steady.

ANTARYĀMĪ The indwelling guide.

ANTYA-LĪLĀ Later pastimes. Specifically refers to Śrīman
Mahāprabhu's pastimes in Jagannātha Purī.

ANUBHĀVA Deliberate bodily movements that correspond with one's dominant spiritual emotion.

ĀNUKŪLYA-ABHILĀṢA The desire to serve Kṛṣṇa favorably.

APARĀDHA Offense.

APRATIHATĀ Unbroken or uninterrupted. Refers to *bhakti* that is undeterred.

ARCANA Ritualistic worship of the Deity.

ARTHA That which is considered of value and worthy of pursuit. Refers to wealth, power, or worldly position.

ĀSAKTI Attachment. Refers to the last stage of *sādhana-bhakti*, wherein attachment for the object of one's love (Kṛṣṇa) awakens.

ASURA An ungodly, selfish person.

ĀTMĀ The self, body, mind, or, more commonly, the soul.

ĀTMĀRĀMA Self-satisfied.

ĀTYANTIKĪ Unlimited.

AVATĀRA An incarnation of God.

ĀVEŚA Absorption in or empowerment by God.

AYOGA Separation from Kṛṣṇa.

BADDHA-JĪVA A materially bound soul.

BHAGAVĀN God, possessor of all opulences (wealth, strength, fame, beauty, knowledge, and renunciation).

BHAJANA Internal culture of love of God.

BHAJANA-KRIYĀ The third stage of *bhakti*, in which one begins to perform devotional practices.

BHAKTI-MĀRGA The path of devotion.

BHĀVA Spiritual ecstasy.

BHĀVA-BHAKTA A devotee in whose heart Kṛṣṇa's internal energy has dawned.

BHĀVA-BHAKTI The stage of *bhakti* prior to the attainment of *prema*.

BHĀVA-SĀDHANA The cultivation of the *bhāva-bhakta*'s budding relationship with Kṛṣṇa.

BHĀVOLLĀSA-RATI The romantic sentiment for Kṛṣṇa tasted by the handmaidens of Śrī Rādhā. Also called *mañjarī-bhāva*.

BHŪMI Earth.

BRAHMACĀRĪ A celibate student.

BRAHMA-JÑĀNA Self-realization or knowledge of Brahman.

BRAHMĀLOKA The abode of Brahmā, the secondary creator.

BRAHMAN The existential aspect of the Absolute or the aura of Bhagavān.

BRĀHMAṆA One who knows Brahman. A member of the intellectual, priestly class.

BRAHMĀNANDA The joy one experiences in self-realization.

CAMATKĀRA A sense of intense wonder or astonishment, which is the basis of *bhakti-rasa*.

CATUR-VYŪHA The fourfold expansion of the Lord, consisting of Vāsudeva, Saṅkarṣaṇa, Pradyumna, and Aniruddha.

CETAḤ Mind, heart, or consciousness.

CID-ĀNANDAMAYA Filled with transcendental joy and knowledge.

CIN-MAYA PŪRṆA-TATTVA The complete spiritual reality.

CIT Consciousness or cognizance.

DAINYA Humility.

DĀSYA-BHAKTI Devotion in the mood of a servant.

DHARMA Religion or righteous life.

DĪKṢĀ Initiation in which the *guru* bestows the *mantra* on
the disciple.

GAUṆA-BHAKTI *Bhakti* of an indirect nature, in contrast to
sākṣāt (direct) *bhakti*.

GĀYATRĪ MANTRA The prototype Vedic *mantra*, said to be
the mother of all Vedic *mantras* and meters.

GOPĀLA MANTRA The principal Gauḍīya *dīkṣā mantra*,
which consists of eighteen syllables.

GOPĪ-JANA The cowherd girls of Vraja.

GOSVĀMĪ One who has mastered the sensual and mental urges.

GUṆA Quality. Refers to the three material influences of
sattva, *rajas*, and *tamas*.

GURU The spiritual preceptor.

GURU-PARAMPARĀ The succession of spiritual masters.

HLĀDINĪ-ŚAKTI Śrī Kṛṣṇa's bliss potency.

ĪŚVARA Controller. Often used to denote the Paramātmā,
who is the controller of the material creation.

JAPA-MĀLĀ The rosary of 108 Tulasī beads on which one
chants the names of God.

JĪVA The conscious, eternal, individual living being.

JÑĀNA Knowledge.

JÑĀNA-MĀRGA The spiritual path in which the practitioner cultivates introspection and detachment from the material world with the goal of attaining liberation from material existence.

JÑĀNĪ-BHAKTA One whose *bhakti* includes awareness of God's opulence.

KAITAVA Cheating. Indicates materially motivated religion.

KALI-YUGA The present age of quarrel.

KADAMBA A type of flowering tree in Vṛndāvana.

KĀMA Desire.

KĀMA-GĀYATRĪ An expression of the *gāyatrī mantra* especially designed to awaken romantic love for Kṛṣṇa.

KARMA The cycle of action and reaction within the material plane.

KAUSTUBHA The jewel Śrī Kṛṣṇa wears over his heart, which represents the totality of all *jīvas*.

KIṄKARA A servant.

KĪRTANA Glorification through singing or chanting.

KĪRTI Fame.

KLEŚAGHNĪ The removal of material distress, which is one of the qualities of *sādhana-bhakti*.

KṚṢṆA-PREMA Love of Kṛṣṇa.

KUMUDA Lotus flower.

LĀLASĀMAYĪ A type of prayer where the devotee prays with longing to attain a specific goal: for example, a specific service to the Lord.

LĪLĀ The divine play of Bhagavān.

LĪLĀ-SEVĀ Service performed within the Lord's pastimes.

LĪLĀ-SMARAṆA Remembrance of Kṛṣṇa's pastimes.

LOBHA Greed. Refers to sacred greed, which is the basis for engaging in the practice of *rāgānugā-bhakti*.

MĀDANĀKHYA-MAHĀBHĀVA The love Śrī Rādhā tastes in union with Kṛṣṇa.

MĀDHURYA Sweetness.

MĀDHURYA-RASA Romantic love of Kṛṣṇa.

MAHĀBHĀVA Great ecstasy, the highest point to which *prema-bhakti* can rise.

MAHĀBHĀVA-SVARŪPINĪ The personification of the highest love, Śrī Rādhā.

MAHĀŚAYA A greatly respectable person.

MAHĀTMĀ A great soul.

MAHAT-TATTVA The aggregate of the unmanifest material elements.

MĀNA Jealous anger or the separation that occurs when lovers quarrel with one another.

MAṄGALA Auspicious or fortunate.

MAṄGALĀCARAṆA The auspicious invocation appearing at the beginning of sacred texts.

MAÑJARĪ A maidservant of Śrī Rādhā.

MAÑJARĪ-BHĀVA The sentiment of the maidservants of Śrī Rādhā.

MANTRA A mystical formula of words intended to deliver one from the limits of one's own mind and awaken love of God.

MANTRA-DHYĀNA Meditation on one's *guru*-given *mantra*.

MĀYĀ The illusion within which conditioned souls are enmeshed.

MĀYĀ-ŚAKTI The illusory energy of Bhagavān.

MIŚRA-SATTVA A condition of existence in which the soul identifies with matter.

MOKṢA-LAGHUTĀKṚT That which makes light of liberation. One of the qualities of *bhāva-bhakti*.

MUKTI Liberation from material existence.

NAIṢṬHIKĪ-BHAKTI Fixed devotion.

NĀMA Name.

NAMASKĀRA To offer respects.

NĀMA-APARĀDHA Offense to the holy name.

NĀMA-BHAJANA Internal worship of the holy name.

NĀMA-DHARMA The spiritual path centered on the chanting of the holy name.

NĀMA-MANTRA A *mantra* comprised of God's names. Specifically refers to the Hare Kṛṣṇa *mahā-mantra*.

NĀMA-SĀDHANA The practice of chanting the name of God.

NĀMA-SAṄKĪRTANA Glorification of God through singing his names.

NĀMA-ŚREṢṬHAM The highest ideal realized in relation to the chanting of God's name.

NIRHETU Without cause.

NIṢKĀMA-KARMA-YOGA Forgoing the fruits of one's actions in the culture of God consciousness.

NIṢṬHĀ Steadiness. Refers to the stage of *bhakti* that follows *anartha-nivṛtti* and precedes *ruci*.

NIṢṬHITĀ BHAJANA-KRIYĀ Steady, uninterrupted *sādhana-bhakti*.

NITYA-LĪLĀ The eternal pastimes of Kṛṣṇa in Goloka.

NITYA-SIDDHA PARIKARA An eternally perfect associate of the Lord.

OṀ The primordial sound vibration that pervades all existence. A name for God.

PAÑCAMA-PURUṢĀRTHA The fifth goal of human life, Mahāprabhu's conception of *prema-bhakti*.

PARAMĀTMĀ The oversoul of the material creation.

PĀRAKA-BRAHMA NĀMA The name that can deliver one to the highest conception of spirituality.

PARAMA-PRAKṚTI Supreme energy.

PARAMA-PURUṢA Supreme person.

PARAṀ BRAHMAN Supreme Brahman.

PARAMEŚVARA Supreme controller.

PRAJÑA Wisdom.

PRAKAṬA-LĪLĀ Śrī Kṛṣṇa's earthly pastimes.

PRAKṚTI Material nature.

PRAMĀṆA A source of evidence.

PRAṆĀMA To offer respects.

PRĀṆA Life air.

PRAṆAVA OṀKĀRA The primeval syllable "Oṁ."

PRĀṆEŚVARA The Lord of one's life.

PRĀPTY-ABHILĀṢA The desire to attain the association of Kṛṣṇa.

PRĀRABDHA-KARMA The *karma* that is presently manifest in the form of one's body and mind.

PRATIṢṬHĀ The desire for worldly position or prestige. A major obstacle to the attainment of pure *bhakti*.

PRAVĀSA The separation that occurs when lovers are separated by distance and time.

PRAYOJANA-TATTVA The metaphysical truth concerning the nature of the goal of spiritual discipline.

PRAYOJANA-TATTVĀCĀRYA The teacher who exemplifies and explains the goal of spiritual discipline. For Gauḍīyas, this is Raghunātha Dāsa Gosvāmī.

PREMA Love of God.

PREMA-BHAKTI The highest stage of devotion: love of God.

PREMA-DHARMA The path of love of Kṛṣṇa.

PREMA-RASA The unprecedented taste of love of God.

PREMA-SAṄKĪRTANA Congregational chanting of the name of Kṛṣṇa in love of God.

PREMA-VAICITTYA The feeling of separation that occurs when lovers are in the presence of one another yet fear impending separation.

PRIYA-NARMA-SAKHĀ A friend of Śrī Kṛṣṇa who is involved to some extent in his amorous pastimes with the cowherd girls of Vṛndāvana.

PŪRṆA Full or complete.

PŪRṆĀNANDA-MAYA Of the nature of complete bliss.

PURUṢA Person.

PURUṢĀRTHA The goals of human life: *dharma, artha, kāma,* and *mokṣa.*

PURUṢĀVATĀRA The three incarnations of Viṣṇu who create and maintain the material creation.

PŪRVAPAKṢA In classical Vedāntic discussions, the antithesis of a stated thesis.

PŪRVA-RĀGA The separation lovers feel before they actually meet and formally acknowledge their love for one another.

RĀDHĀ-DĀSYA Service to Śrī Rādhā. *Rādhā-dāsya* is synonymous with *bhāvollāsa-rati*.

RĀGA Attachment (to Kṛṣṇa) or a state of intensification of *prema*.

RĀGĀNUGĀ-BHAKTI The practice of *bhakti* following in the footsteps of those in whom attachment to Kṛṣṇa is inborn (*rāgātmikās*).

RĀGĀNUGA-SĀDHANA The practice of following the mood of the residents of Vṛndāvana.

RĀGA-MĀRGA The path of spontaneous love of Kṛṣṇa.

RAJAS The material mode of passion.

RĀJA A king.

RĀJA-VIDYĀ The king of knowledge or knowledge of kings, which in either case refers to *bhakti*.

RASA Aesthetic rapture in love of God.

RĀSA-PAÑCĀDHYĀYA The five chapters of *Śrīmad-Bhāgavatam* describing Śrī Kṛṣṇa's dance of love with the cowherd girls of Vṛndāvana.

RASĀNANDA The bliss experienced when tasting aesthetic rapture in love of God.

RASĀNTARĀVEŚA Internally absorbed in aesthetic rapture.

RASARĀJA The king of sacred aesthetic rapture. Refers to Śrī Kṛṣṇa.

RATI A synonym for *bhāva-bhakti*.

RUCI Taste.

RUCI-BHAKTI The stage of *bhakti* after *niṣṭhā* and before *āsakti*, wherein the devotee has taste for the practices of *bhakti*, such as hearing and chanting about Kṛṣṇa.

SAD-GURU Eternal spiritual preceptor.

SĀDHANA Spiritual practice.

SĀDHANA-BHAKTI The stage of *bhakti* in practice.

SĀDHANA-SĀDHYA-TATTVA The metaphysical truth concerning the practice of *bhakti* (*sādhana*) and the goal of practice (*sādhya*).

SĀDHAKA Practitioner.

SĀDHAKA-DEHA The practitioner's body.

SĀDHU A saintly person.

SĀDHU-SAṄGA The second stage of *bhakti*: association with saints.

SĀDHYA The goal to be attained from a given spiritual practice.

SAHETU With good reason.

SAKHĪ Female friend.

SAKHYA-RASA Fraternal love for Kṛṣṇa.

SĀKṢĀT BHAKTI-VARTINI Steadiness in *bhakti* itself, as opposed to steadiness in that which is favorable to *bhakti*.

ŚAKTI Energy.

ŚAKTIMĀN Energetic source (God).

SAMARTHĀ-RATI Competent love. Refers to the love of Śrī

Rādhā, which is competent to subdue and control Śrī Kṛṣṇa.

SAMBANDHA Relationship.

SAMBANDHA-JÑĀNA A conceptual orientation to Kṛṣṇa *bhakti*: metaphysical knowledge about the nature of the relationship between God and the world, God and the individual souls, and the individual souls and the world.

SAMBHOGA In *mādhurya-rasa*, the meeting between Kṛṣṇa and his beloved.

SAMPRADĀYA A spiritual lineage.

SAMPRĀRTHANAMAYĪ Prayers of submission to the Lord.

SAMSĀRA The cycle of birth and death.

SAMŚAYA A doubt.

SAMVIT-ŚAKTI The Lord's cognitive potency.

SANDHINĪ-ŚAKTI The Lord's existential potency.

SĀNDRĀNANDA-VIŚEṢĀTMĀ The condensed bliss that is one of the qualities of *prema-bhakti*.

SAṄKĪRTANA Collective glorification. See also *nāma-saṅkīrtana*.

SANNYĀSA Renunciation of the world.

ŚARAṆĀGATI Surrender.

ŚĀSTRA Revealed scripture.

SAT Eternal.

SATTVA The material mode of goodness.

SĀTTVIKA-BHĀVA Involuntary bodily transformations resulting from spiritual emotion. One of the ingredients of *rasa*.

SAUHĀRDA-ABHILĀṢA The desire for the friendship of the Lord.

SIDDHĀNTA Philosophical conclusion.

SIDDHA-DEHA The spiritual body with which the devotee serves Śrī Kṛṣṇa in his eternal pastimes.

ŚLOKA A verse from scripture.

SMARAṆA Remembrance or meditation.

SNEHA Affection.

ŚRADDHĀ Faith. The first stage of *bhakti*.

ŚREYAḤ Most auspicious. Specifically refers to the fourfold auspiciousness that characterizes pure devotion in the stage of *ruci*.

ŚRĪ-KṚṢṆĀKARṢIṆĪ One of the qualities of *prema-bhakti*: it has the power to attract Śrī Kṛṣṇa himself.

SṚṢṬI-LĪLĀ Mahā-Viṣṇu's play of creating the material plane of existence.

ŚRUTI The *Vedas* and *Upaniṣads*.

STHĀYI-BHĀVA The dominant spiritual sentiment through which one desires to serve Kṛṣṇa in his eternal pastimes.

ŚUBHADĀ Auspiciousness, one of the qualities of *sādhana-bhakti*.

ŚUDDHA-BHAKTI Pure *bhakti*, not encumbered by *jñāna* and *karma*.

ŚUDDHA-SATTVA Pure spiritual existence.

ŚUDDHA-SATTVA-VIŚEṢĀTMĀ The arising of God's internal energy within the heart of the devotee when *bhāva-bhakti* awakens.

SU-DURLABHĀ Very rarely attained. Refers to *bhāva-bhakti*.

SU-MEDHASA Very intelligent. Usually refers to those who take up the process of *nāma-saṅkīrtana*.

SŪTRA A terse philosophical aphorism.

SVĀHĀ Sacrifice.

SVAKĪYA-VĀDA The theological idea that Rādhā and Kṛṣṇa are married in their eternal pastimes.

SVARŪPA One's spiritual form or nature.

SVARŪPĀNANDA The bliss of absorption in one's spiritual form.

SVARŪPA-LAKṢAṆA The primary or intrinsic characteristic of a given object.

SVARŪPA-ŚAKTI God's internal potency.

SVARŪPA-ŚAKTYĀNANDA The bliss of being absorbed in Śrī Kṛṣṇa's internal energy.

SVARŪPĀVEŚA Absorption in one's spiritual form.

SVARŪPA-SIDDHI The perfection of identifying with one's spiritual form.

ŚYĀMA A blackish color that according to Indian aesthetic literature corresponds with the emotion of amorous love.

TAD-ANUKŪLA-VASTU-VARTINI Steadiness in that which is favorable to *bhakti*.

TAD-BHĀVECCHĀMAYĪ The identification Rādhā's handmaidens have with her by which they are able to taste her love.

TAMAS The material mode of ignorance.

TANTRA That which expands the meaning of the *Vedas*.

TĀRAKA-BRAHMA NĀMA The name that can deliver one from material existence.

TAṬASTHA-LAKṢAṆA The marginal characteristics of a given object.

TATTVA A metaphysical truth.

UDDĪPANA-VIBHĀVA That which stimulates the tasting of
  rasa.

UTKAṆṬHĀ *Sakhya-rasa*'s equivalent of *pūrva-rāga*.

UTTAMA-ADHIKĀRĪ A superlative devotee.

VAIDHĪ-BHAKTI Regulative devotional service. Also refers
  to the path of *bhakti* in which the goal is the worship of
  Lakṣmī-Nārāyaṇa in Vaikuṇṭha.

VAIDHĪ-SĀDHANA The practices of regulative devotional
  service.

VASTU-NIRDEŚA A verse at the beginning of a book that
  defines what the book is about.

VĀTSALYA Parental love of Kṛṣṇa.

VIBHĀVA That which stimulates *bhāva*, causing it to rise to
  the intensity of aesthetic rapture in love of God.

VIDYĀ Knowledge.

VIPRALAMBHA The love in separation that is exclusive to
  mādhurya-rasa.

VIPRALAMBHA-MŪRTI The form of separation, an epithet
  given to Śrīman Mahāprabhu during his pastimes in
  Jagannātha Purī.

VIRAHA-BHĀVA The ecstasy of love in separation.

VIŚUDDHA-SATTVA Pure spiritual existence.

VIṢAYA An object or, in classical Vedāntic discussion, the
  strengthening of the doubt.

VIṢĀDA Despair, despondence, or remorse.

VYABHICĀRĪ-BHĀVA Transitory emotions that rise from the ocean of one's dominant spiritual sentiment, nourish it, and then recede back into it.

YOGA Union. Specifically refers to the union of the devotee and Kṛṣṇa in love.

YOGA-MĀYĀ The aspect of Śrī Kṛṣṇa's internal potency that enables him to forget that he is God and thus enjoy intimate relationships with his devotees.

YUGA A long period of time. Specifically refers to each of the four ages of Vedic cosmology: Satya, Tretā, Dvāpara, and Kali.

YUGĀVATĀRA A specific descent of the Lord in a given *yuga*.

YUGA-DHARMA The scripturally recommended religious process for a given *yuga*.

māyā-śakti, 83
mercy, 82
mind, 15–16, 67
miśra-sattva, 15
mokṣa, 65–70
    See also liberation; *mukti*
mokṣa-laghutākṛt, 21–22
mukti, 13, 55, 95, 138
    See also liberation; *mokṣa*

nāma-aparādha, 53
nāma-bhajana, 39, 40
nāma-mantra, 13, 83, 100, 102
nāma-saṅkīrtana. *See saṅkīrtana*
nāma-smaraṇam, 31
nāma-śreṣṭham, 18
names of God, 18, 28–30
    See also Kṛṣṇa *nāma*
Nārada, 108
Nārāyaṇa, 13
Narottama dāsa Ṭhākura, 17, 86
nirhetu, 125
niṣkāma-karma-yoga, 15
niṣṭha. *See niṣṭhitā bhajana-kriyā*
niṣṭhitā bhajana-kriyā, 17, 46,
    49–58, 64, 68, 71, 77
nitya-līlā, 73, 137
Nityānanda Prabhu, 74

offenses, 39, 40, 57
    See also aparādha

Padyāvalī, IX, 7, 110
pañcama-puruṣārtha, 70
Paramātmā, 72–73
    See also antaryāmī
pleasure, 66–67
    See also ānanda; kāma
power, 66–67. *See also artha*

Prabodhānanda Sarasvatī, 20
prakaṭa-līlā, 113, 115
prāṇa, 73, 94–95
praṇaya, 115, 140, 141
prāpty-abhilāṣa, 72
Prārthanā, 132
Pratāparudra Mahārāja, 12–13
pratiṣṭhā, 39. *See also* pride
pravāsa, 112
prayer, 64, 73, 82, 135, 137
prayojana, 46, 100
prema, 108–9, 110, 112–13, 114
    and *bhajana*, 86
    and *bhāva-bhakti*, 94, 99–100
    and humility, 49, 122–23
    and knowledge, 19–20, 32, 124
    and love, 22–23
    and *nāma-saṅkīrtana*, 13
    and *rasa*, 127
    and *sādhaka-deha*, 138
    and separation, 22
    and service, 123–24
    and spiritual identity, 23, 123
    and *sthāyi-bhāva*, 140
    as the sun of love of God, 99
    beginning of, 48–49, 72
    distribution of, 6, 12–13
    effects of, 116
    eligibility for, 57–58
    higher than God, 126–29
    leads to postliberated life, 70
    of Rādhā, 6–7, 12, 122–23, 127
    of Vraja, 74–75, 87
    seven steps towards, 14
Prema Bhakti-candrikā, 138
prema-dharma, 46, 69–70
prema-saṅkīrtana. *See saṅkīrtana*
prema-vaicittya, 112
prerakaḥ, 20